To Jasmine,
Thanks for the sup,
Continued Blessings &
Success!
ORedd

Happy Birthday to you for the support and advice. Lynn & Lenord & Johanna & Lucas

Speed Reader

RIGHTEOUSNESS,
THE REMIX- TURN UP THE VOLUME ON GOD !

A NO-PRESSURE GUIDE TO
BUILDING YOUR SPIRITUALITY.

O. REDD

authorHOUSE

AuthorHouse™
1663 Liberty Drive
Bloomington, IN 47403
www.authorhouse.com
Phone: 1 (800) 839-8640

© 2017 O.Redd. All rights reserved.
Photographs by Stephen Kinstler

No part of this book may be reproduced, stored in a retrieval system, or transmitted by any means without the written permission of the author.

GOD'S WORD Translation (GW)
Copyright © 1995 by God's Word to the Nations.
Used by permission of Baker Publishing Group

Published by AuthorHouse 05/26/2017

ISBN: 978-1-5246-5996-7 (sc)
ISBN: 978-1-5246-5994-3 (hc)
ISBN: 978-1-5246-5995-0 (e)

Library of Congress Control Number: 2017900642

Print information available on the last page.

Any people depicted in stock imagery provided by Thinkstock are models, and such images are being used for illustrative purposes only. Certain stock imagery © Thinkstock.

This book is printed on acid-free paper.

Because of the dynamic nature of the Internet, any web addresses or links contained in this book may have changed since publication and may no longer be valid. The views expressed in this work are solely those of the author and do not necessarily reflect the views of the publisher, and the publisher hereby disclaims any responsibility for them.

Scriptures marked AMP are quotations taken from the Amplified® Bible, Copyright © 1954, 1958, 1962, 1964, 1965, 1987 by The Lockman Foundation Used by permission. (www.Lockman.org)

The ESV® Bible (The Holy Bible, English Standard Version®) copyright © 2001 by Crossway, a publishing ministry of Good News Publishers. ESV® Text Edition: 2011. The ESV® text has been reproduced in cooperation with and by permission of Good News Publishers. Unauthorized reproduction of this publication is prohibited. All rights reserved.

Scriptures noted GW are taken from GOD'S WORD®, © 1995 God's Word to the Nations. Used by permission of Baker Publishing Group.

Scripture quotations marked HCSB are taken from the Holman Christian Standard Bible®, Copyright © 1999, 2000, 2002, 2003, 2009 by Holman Bible Publishers. Used by permission. Holman Christian Standard Bible®, Holman CSB®, and HCSB® are federally registered trademarks of Holman Bible Publishers.

Scripture noted ISV taken from the Holy Bible: International Standard Version® Release 2.0. Copyright © 1996-2012 by the ISV Foundation. Used by permission of Davidson Press, LLC. ALL RIGHTS RESERVED INTERNATIONALLY.

Scripture quotations marked "KJV" are taken from the Holy Bible, King James Version, Cambridge, 1769

Scripture marked NKJV taken from the New King James Version®. Copyright © 1982 by Thomas Nelson, Inc. Used by permission. All rights reserved.

Scripture noted NASB taken from the NEW AMERICAN STANDARD BIBLE®, Copyright © 1960,1962,1963,1968,1971,1972,1973,1975,1977,1995 by The Lockman Foundation. Used by permission.

Scriptures marked NIV taken from THE HOLY BIBLE, NEW INTERNATIONAL VERSION®, NIV® Copyright © 1973, 1978, 1984, 2011 by Biblica, Inc.® Used by permission. All rights reserved worldwide.

Scripture quotations marked "NLT" are taken from the Holy Bible, New Living Translation, copyright 1996. Used by permission of Tyndale House Publishers, Inc., Wheaton, Illinois 60189. All rights reserved

Scriptures noted NLV taken from The Holy Bible, New Life Version © Christian Literature International
Christian Literature International (CLI) is a non-profit ministry dedicated to publishing and providing the Word of God in a form that can be read and understood by new readers and the well-educated alike... and at an affordable price. We invite you to learn how the NEW LIFE Version unlocks the treasures of God's Word!

This book is dedicated to my mom, dad and grandmother. Thank you for encouraging my dreams and supporting my creativity. I couldn't have done this without you. I love you! -Redd

"Jesus Christ is the same yesterday and today and forever" Hebrews 13:8(NIV).

"It's not the word of God that changes…but the way it's presented that sometimes has to."- O.Redd

TABLE OF CONTENTS

Introduction xi

Section 1.   Accepting God's Love *1*

Chapter 1.   You Are Approved! 3
Chapter 2.   Unconditional Love 11
Chapter 3.   Just The Way You Are! 21

Section 2.   Communicating with God *35*

Chapter 4.   Get to Know God 37
Chapter 5.   Come and Talk to Me 44
Chapter 6.   Watch, Hope and Expect 51

Section 3.   The Power of Positivity *61*

Chapter 7.   Discover the Positive! 63
Chapter 8.   Watch Your Words! 70
Chapter 9.   Stop, Look & Listen 79

Section 4.   Spiritual Warfare *89*

Chapter 10. The Battle Within 91
Chapter 11. Power and Authority 99
Chapter 12. The Full Armor 110

Section 5.   Fight the Fear! *129*

Chapter 13. Inside the Fear 131
Chapter 14. Dare to Believe! 143

Chapter 15. Enjoy Your Life!... 158

Section 6.   This is the Remix! *171*
Chapter 16. Jesus, the Rebel... 173
Chapter 17. Invite God to the Party!... 191
About the Author 203

INTRODUCTION

"For the LORD is good. His unfailing love continues forever, and his faithfulness continues to each generation"(Psalm 100:5, NLT).

I am not a preacher. I haven't been to Bible College. I don't have any degrees in ministry. I don't even attend church on Sunday. Yet, here you are holding a book that I've written about God and how to strengthen your spirituality. Pretty strange, huh? Actually, the fact that I don't have any of those degrees or titles will probably help me in the long run. I believe it shows how real God is, how He is able to use absolutely anyone and that He does indeed have a sense of humor.

Now, you may be thinking, *"So, who are you and why should I listen to anything you have to say…especially about God?"* Believe it or not, when I started writing this book…I asked myself the exact same thing. Why should anyone listen to me?

I wasn't raised in church. I haven't always been particularly spiritual. I'm a guy who loves music, who writes songs, who raps and has performed on stage since I was a teenager.

I've spent my whole life being focused and determined to follow my dreams of being in the entertainment industry. I've won contests, talent shows, publish my own music, have songs on iTunes, have been nominated for awards and have come very close to seeing those dreams come true. So, why would I put all of that on hold to write a book about God…when I don't even go to church?

I have to admit; it didn't make much sense to me at first either.

However, there's something you should know about me. Even though I wear my hats backward, my pants a little too low, play my music loud and will probably be judged for all those things...I am a Christian.

No, I didn't develop my relationship with God by going to church on Sunday. I don't have a closet full of suits from the Steve Harvey Collection. I don't like to wake up early, dress up or be around a lot of people when I'm trying to learn. So, I knew if I wanted a relationship with God, I would have to find different ways to learn and build one with Him.

I know you might be thinking, *"Wait a minute...doesn't the Bible say we're supposed to go to church?"* Yes, the Bible stresses the importance of assembling together to hear the word of God and learn to obey it, (Deuteronomy 31:12-13). However, that can be done anywhere.

It's obvious from the way Jesus traveled around preaching and healing in small towns, by rivers and even in people's homes that God doesn't have a particular address.

The scripture tells us we should let the word of Christ dwell richly *in* us (Colossians 3:16) and in Matthew 18:20 (NIV), the Lord says, *"For where two or three gather in my name, there am I with them."*

Well, that's exactly what we're doing right now as you're holding this book! We're gathering together in God's name and inviting Him into the fold.

Too many people confuse going to church on Sunday with having a relationship with God. They are often two *very* different things.

Going to church is a great way to hear the Word of God, fellowship with others, get pointed in the right direction and learn. However, it isn't the *only* way to learn.

Going to church is a great way for people to be motivated, encouraged and inspired to grow closer to God. However, going doesn't automatically give you a relationship with The Lord...the pastor, maybe...but not The Lord. What matters is the work you put into pursuing that relationship *after* you leave the building.

It's not like going to Wal-Mart where you can get everything you need under one roof at one time!

I have always believed that. So, when I wanted to develop my relationship with God, I decided to jump into it head first and start doing the work. I found ways to study, spend time with Him and make Him a part of my life.

Obviously, what happened next was pretty amazing since I felt the need to write a whole book about it.

However, I have to be honest with you... writing this book was never part of my plan. I was completely happy following my dreams of being in the music industry and keeping my relationship with The Lord, the lessons I was learning and my spirituality to myself. Obviously, He had other plans.

As I was growing in my relationship with The Lord, I started sharing a little of that experience with the people closest to me. As I became more comfortable opening up and talking about my spirituality, other people became comfortable opening up as well. Although, what I found out was pretty disheartening.

I saw the many misconceptions people had about God and what it means to be a Christian. I saw how many people thought living for God is all about what you "can't" and "aren't" supposed to do.

I saw how people didn't want anything to do with God because of what goes on in some churches or how some Christians behave. I saw how certain types of Christians were giving God a bad name and were doing more damage to His Kingdom than good.

I learned many reasons why people, even those who go to church, didn't have the type of relationship with God or the victory in their lives that they wanted.

I saw how people let their shortcomings, bad habits or the lives they lead keep them from having a relationship with God. The list went on and on and none of it was true of the God I was getting to know.

So, the more I learned, the more I shared with others around me and was pretty amazed at some of the changes I saw take place.

It was then that God spoke to me and said, *"You know I'm not teaching you all of these things for you to keep them to yourself, right?"*

Well, I knew I couldn't go around and talk to everyone in the world... yet. But, the one thing I have always been able to do well ...is write. So, God said, *"Write a book."*

So, that's what I did.

I wrote this book for anyone who has ever felt lost spiritually, out of place or unworthy of God's love. I wrote this book for anyone who has ever been dismissed or looked at as less than spiritual because they don't go to church. I wrote this book for those who really don't know where they fit in or don't have any idea how to start to develop a relationship with the very God who created them.

I wrote this book for people who have gone to church, realized that particular way of learning is not for them and are looking for other ways to build their relationship with God. I wrote this book for those who already have a great relationship with Him to use as a powerful tool to help remind them of all the love and authority He has given us. We can never hear enough of that!

I even wrote this book for those who might not be sure whether or not they believe in God at all…if nothing more than to let them know that *He* believes in *them*!

In this book, I share some of the most important lessons that have helped me develop a strong, powerful, exciting, and fun relationship with God. I'll show you step by step how to build that type of relationship from the ground up.

So, again...why should you listen to me or believe anything I have to say in this book? Three words…*Because. It. Works!*

I have seen it work in my life as well as the lives of others and now I want it to work for you!

No matter your level of spirituality, whether you're fifteen years old or fifty, whether you go to church every Sunday or have never even stepped foot in one...what you are about to read will help you change your life and grow closer to God. I know it did for me!

For those of you not familiar with the term *"Remix"*, it's when a producer or artist takes a song and adds their own spin to it …presenting it in a fresh, new and different way.

When deciding on a title for this book, *Righteousness …the Remix* came to me because it's time for people to see having God in their life as the most fresh, new and exciting experience they'll ever have.

It is my hope that this book helps at least one person see God in a different way and helps them learn to develop an awesome and powerful relationship with Him.

Hebrews 13:8 (NLT) tells us *"Jesus Christ is the same yesterday, today and forever."*

So, it's not the Word of God that changes, but the way it's presented that sometimes has to. And, this is the Remix.

SECTION 1
ACCEPTING GOD'S LOVE

CHAPTER 1

YOU ARE APPROVED!

"This High Priest of ours understands our weaknesses, for he faced all of the same testings we do, yet he did not sin. So let us come boldly to the throne of our gracious God. There we will receive his mercy, and we will find grace to help us when we need it most" (Hebrews 4:15-16, NLT).

God created you for a reason. The things that interest you, the things you are passionate about or like to do, your talent and abilities, the dreams you have for the future, the goals you want to accomplish, even where you are right now in your life as you are reading this book...none of these things are mistakes, they all have a purpose.

God created every one of us in His image and has a great plan for each one of our lives. That plan is for us to have power, walk in victory, live in peace, abundance, prosperity and to see all the great things He has in store for us come to be. However, many people will never get a chance to see these things happen or experience life this way. Many people will never develop a relationship with God, become the person they were created to be, see their dreams come true or learn to live a victorious life simply for one reason; they don't believe they can.

As for *why* some people don't believe they can, the reasons could be endless. Some people believe that the above scripture from Hebrews, where we are told to come boldly to the throne of God, comes with absurd conditions or is meant only for certain types of people. Some people believe when the Bible speaks of God's blessings and promises, it means blessings and promises for everyone but them. Others think they could never live up to the unrealistic standards many Christians pretend to live by. While others are scared off by what they think they will have to give up.

Whatever the reason, many people are afraid to invite Jesus into their lives and get to know God. However, Hebrews 4:15-16 tells us not only can we come to God...but we can come to Him boldly! The word "bold" means *"showing an ability to take risks; being confident and courageous."* (Merriam –Webster.com)

To put aside any doubts, fear or hesitation we may have to begin a relationship with God requires us to do just that; be bold, confident and courageous. Being afraid only holds us back from becoming the person God created us to be and having all He created us to have.

No matter if you are just starting your spiritual journey, have never given it any thought or have been on your path for years, being bold is an important part of moving forward in your relationship with God.

Nevertheless, there are many people who don't feel bold or courageous when it comes to God. There are many people who don't feel comfortable praying or asking God to bless them. There are even people who look at letting God into their lives as a "risk".

In this chapter, "You Are Approved!" I want to begin discussing some of the reasons people feel this way and help people understand that despite whatever it is that may be holding them back, we are already approved to move forward, boldly and courageously in our relationship with God!

I named this chapter, "You Are Approved!" because Romans 4:25 (GWT) tells us, *"Jesus, our Lord, was handed over to death because of our failures and was brought back to life so that we could receive God's approval."*

No matter where you are with your spirituality, I'm sure you have at least heard of the sacrifice Jesus made for us when He died for our sins. His sacrifice was so great, it's all that we need to, *right now*, be able to come to God and pursue our spirituality boldly and with confidence. But, what does that mean?

It means even though we are not perfect and probably never will be, we are already approved to pray bold prayers and ask God for great things. It means we are approved to look past our shortcomings and press forward towards becoming the person God says we can be. It means we are approved to disregard all of the silly conditions and circumstances people put on what it means to be a believer, and find out what that means for ourselves.

So, why do some people still not see this as the exiting opportunity that it is? Why do some people have crosses hanging from their chains and necklaces, in their homes, on bumper stickers and even as tattoos but have a hard time accepting the priceless gift of love it represents?

One reason people feel this way is because they believe God's love and approval is something they have to try and earn. Many people have been led to believe that God's love for us is based on how well we behave. Thinking this way keeps people in fear that they are always doing something that God disapproves of. Feeling this way makes people afraid to come to God boldly and with confidence like the scripture says. Many people don't understand this is not the way it works. God's love for us is not based on how well we behave. If it were... we would all be in trouble!

While God may not always love some of the things we say or do, He loves us because we are His children. There is a big difference! There is no mistake we could ever make or any path we could ever walk down that would make God turn His back on us.

Because we are His children, we can come to Him at any time boldly and with confidence and begin a relationship with Him. Some people don't know this or have been told differently. Many people don't understand that one of the greatest gifts given to us by Jesus is the ability to have God's grace, power, love and mercy on our side, even as we are learning, growing and making mistakes.

Honestly, it's pretty easy to understand why some people may feel this way. God offers us such a great benefits package that sometimes our minds have trouble understanding how good He really is.

As human beings, we are used to a system of having to earn things. This is just the way the way the world operates. Since we were children, most of us have heard, *"If you eat all your food, you can have dessert." "If you study hard enough, you will get good grades." "If you work hard enough, you will get the promotion."* It seems like we are always in the process of trying to earn something.

You have to work hard to earn the love of the person you choose to be with and even some of your own family members. However, many people apply this idea to their relationship with The Lord as well. Many people are afraid to invite God into their lives because they feel they could never do enough good to earn the right to do so.

This may be how the world works. However, John 16:33 tells us that Jesus overcame the world, so God's love for us does not depend on anything we have to earn. Also, John 1: 17 (ESV) tells us, *"For while the Law was given through Moses; grace and truth came through Jesus Christ."*

"Grace" (in this instance) means *"the love and mercy given to us by God because God desires us to have it, not because of anything we have done to earn it."* Other definitions include the words "credit", "favor" and "honor" and almost every definition uses the word "undeserved".

Can you imagine having God's unearned and undeserved favor, credit, honor and blessings, just by living in His presence? Well, that's exactly what His grace is ...and it's available to each one of us *right now*! No matter where we are in our lives, God is eager to give us His grace, power, favor and honor without us worrying about having to earn it.

This can be seen in Ephesians 2:4-9 (NLV) which tells us, *"God has so much loving-kindness. He loves us with such a great love. Even when we were dead because of our sins, He made us alive by what Christ did for us. You have been saved from the punishment of sin by His loving favor. God raised us up from death when He raised up Christ Jesus. He has given us a place with Christ in the Heavens. He did this to show us through all the time to come, the great riches of His loving favor. He has shown us His kindness through Christ Jesus. It is not by anything you have done. It is a gift of God. It is not given to you because you worked for it."*

It's sad to think that many people will never experience God's grace in their lives because they take on the impossible task of trying to earn it. Remember, you may have to try and earn favor with people, but you never have to try and earn it with God!

Think about it this way, if you have company coming over that you're trying to impress, the first thing you may think is, *"I have to clean up the house."* You may rush around vacuuming, dusting, picking clothes up off the floor and washing dishes. By the time you finish trying to prepare, you're too tired and worn out to have anyone over at all.

Well, many people go about pursuing a relationship with God the exact same way! They exhaust themselves by running around trying to clean up their lives before they feel like they can invite God in. The idea of having to do this can overwhelm people and scare them away from ever trying to develop a relationship with God at all.

Whether it's trying to have perfect behavior, quitting bad habits or even giving up certain things like listening to your favorite music, many people feel like there is some big thing they have to do to before they invite God into their lives. I have even heard people say, "Once I get myself together, then I'll work on my relationship with The Lord."

This makes no sense! It's like going to the doctor *after* you get over being sick. If you could cure yourself, then there would be no need for the doctor …right?

Thinking this way is a no- win situation. It puts people on a never-ending cycle of trying to "prepare" themselves for God. People try to "clean up" as much of their life as they can, end up falling short and start to think, *"Well there's no use, I'll never get it right. There's no way God will have anything to do with me!"*

This sort of thinking keeps people from ever coming boldly and confidently to the throne like we are told to in Hebrews 4:15-16. It's a burden that is impossible for us to bear and one that Jesus already carried so we wouldn't have to!

Hebrews 4:15-16 tells us Jesus understands everything we go through. He understands our fears, our temptations and our weaknesses. He understands them all because He faced them Himself, yet did not sin. When He died on the cross, He took all of our sins and weakness upon Himself. He paid the price for our approval with God. So…why would we feel like we have to continue to earn something that has already been paid for?

I like to think of it this way: if a friend took you out to lunch and paid for your meal, you wouldn't go back to the restaurant the next day with more money and try to pay the tab again. You wouldn't continue to show up day after day with more money and try to pay for a bill that has already been settled. How much sense does that make? You would probably just be thankful and sit back and enjoy the meal, because it was a gift. You wouldn't feel like you had to continue to try and earn a gift that has already been paid for, right?

Well, if we wouldn't do that to a friend who paid for something as small as a meal, then why would we do it to Jesus, who already paid the ultimate price for us to have God's approval? Jesus's sacrifice was enough for us to be able to come to God right now and begin a relationship with Him. We don't have to keep trying to earn that right. That tab has already been paid!

Many of you reading this probably do the same thing I do. After I pay my utility bills, I keep the receipt for a while. Imagine how you would react if the electric company or your cell phone company told you, "You didn't pay for last months bill" when you know you did... and disconnected your service. You would probably grab your receipt so fast heads would spin. I'm sure you would take them the receipt and probably give them a piece of your mind while you were at it.

Well, the next time you feel like God doesn't approve of you, remember Hebrews 4:15- 16 is your receipt! That scripture shows us that Jesus already paid for us to have God's love and approval ...and that's something no one can disconnect us from!

Let's take a look at Luke 10:38-42, the story of Mary and Martha. It's a perfect example of how people are so busy trying to gain approval and "prepare" for The Lord, that they miss out on their experience with Him altogether.

While Jesus and His disciples were traveling, they came to a village where a woman named Martha opened her home to them. Martha had a sister named Mary, who sat at the Lord's feet enjoying His company and listening to everything He said. But, Martha was running around, distracted by all the things she thought she had to do. Maybe Martha felt like she had to clean up, dress a certain way or serve a certain meal to gain favor with The Lord. Finally, all her running around got the best of her.

She came to Jesus and asked, "Lord, don't you care that my sister has left me to do the work by myself? Tell her to help me!"

"*Martha, Martha,*" the Lord answered, "*you are worried and upset about many things, but few things are needed, or indeed only one. Mary has chosen what is better, and it will not be taken away from her*" (Luke 10:40-42, NIV).

Mary decided to sit down and just enjoy being in The Lord's presence, while Martha ran around like a madwoman trying to do everything she thought needed to be done. Mary wasn't concerned with everything Martha thought had to be done in order to invite Jesus in and neither was Jesus.

When Jesus told Martha, "*few things are needed, or indeed only one*", I believe He was telling Martha that the only thing she needed to do was "come and sit".

But, many people are like Martha. They obsess over the things they think they must do in order to gain The Lord's approval and invite Him into their lives. They never give themselves a chance to just "come and sit" in His presence and end up missing the whole experience!

Jesus even tells Martha in the New Living Translation of that verse that she is too concerned with all the "details". There are many Christians who are like Martha. They are so concerned with all the "details" that they miss out on the actual experience of enjoying The Lord in their life. They have to have the right clothes, the right way of speaking, the right circle of friends, the right house, the right car and even the right position in church. Every time I see one of these "Martha's" …I wonder how long it has been since they just chilled out and actually enjoyed spending time with God?

And even worse, they can pass that feeling on to other people! The next time you encounter someone like this, someone who tells you that you have to "do this" and "do that" before you can *boldly* invite God into your life…remind them that "You Are Approved!" and show them your receipt!

Remember, it took a certain degree of boldness and confidence for Mary to just come and sit in the presence of The Lord. Mary came to the throne with the same kind of boldness that we are told to come with in Hebrews 4:15-16 ...and Jesus honored that!

If this is something that has been holding you back from having God in your life and pursuing your spirituality with boldness and confidence, you don't have to continue to think this way! You don't have to continue to be like Martha and run around trying to "prepare" for The Lord or "earn" the approval you already have! In John 6:29 (NIV) Jesus tells us, *"The work of God is this: to believe in the one he has sent."*

If we believe, then God's love and grace is always available to us. We already have His approval along with all the power and benefits of having a relationship with Him through Jesus Christ. There are no amount of good deeds we can do to earn that, just like there is no mistake we can make to ever lose it. It's a gift that has always been there and always will be there. It has already been paid for. It's just up to us when we realize it and decide to put it to use in our lives!

CHAPTER 2

UNCONDITIONAL LOVE

"I am convinced that nothing can ever separate us from God's love. Neither death nor life, neither angels nor demons, neither our fears for today nor our worries about tomorrow— not even the powers of hell can separate us from God's love. No power in the sky above or in the earth below—indeed, nothing in all creation will ever be able to separate us from the love of God that is revealed in Christ Jesus our Lord"(Romans 8:38-39, NLT).

Now that we understand that God's love and approval isn't something we have to try and earn, I want to take a look at some of the other reasons why people may not feel bold or confident when it comes to their relationship with The Lord.

In the conversations I've had with people, many which led me to write this book, two things kept coming up more often than not ...doubt and fear.

While some people walk around believing that they could never do enough good to earn God's love and approval, there are those who are too afraid to even try.

There are many people, some who may be reading this right now, who are too afraid to approach the throne, let alone boldly because they believe God is angry and upset with them. There are countless people who live their lives every day and feel like they have to stay as far away from God as possible because He is "mad" with them for one reason or another.

There are people who live with the image of an angry, judgmental God who watches over us, waiting to scrutinize our every move and shake His finger at everything we do wrong. With all the mistakes we make as human beings, this can cause people to wonder how much God really loves us ...or if He even likes us at all!

Believing that God is "mad" at us scares people away from coming to the throne with boldness and confidence like we are told to in Hebrews 4:15-16.

Many people feel this way because they still have things in their life they need to work on or change. Some may feel this way because they don't live exactly as the Bible says we should. I mean really, the only person who got it completely right was Jesus, and we're not Jesus! We may try to be...but we're not Him. The sooner we realize that, the sooner we can go ahead and let that one go!

Some people feel like God is mad with them because they aren't in church every Sunday or don't go at all. While others have been made to feel this way by other people. (It's sad to say, but coming in contact with someone who claims to be a Christian can actually drive a person further away from God than they were before!)

Whatever the reason, people let doubt and fear become "roadblocks" on their way to the throne. They let doubt and fear stand in their way of having a great relationship with God and believing that He loves us no matter what.

In this chapter, "Unconditional Love", I want to help people understand that we don't have to let these feelings stand in our way of boldly coming to God and having Him in our lives. I want to let people know, no matter what, God loves us unconditionally. He is not "mad" at us over the things we need to work on or change. He is not angry with us because of our shortcomings and flaws. He is not even upset with us over our sins because once we come to Him and truly ask for forgiveness ...even those are forgotten!

Romans 8:38-39 tells us that nothing could ever separate us from God's love. Not death, not life, not angels or demons, not our fears or worries, not even the powers of hell could stop God from loving us!

Now, if you're one of the people who is afraid that God is "mad" at you and doesn't love you ...what was your reason again?

If the fear of God being "angry" with you has been holding you back from having Him in your life or doubting how much you're loved ...you can relax! God already knows everything we need to work on or change about ourselves and He is willing and eager to help us with the process! But, many people will never come to Him because they are too afraid and don't think they can.

As I began my own walk with God, this sort of fear could have stopped me right in my tracks. I still had many things I needed to work on, and still do! I didn't fit the image of what some people thought a Christian should be. I didn't go to church on Sunday, I have tattoos, I cuss, used bad language and had a quick temper. I would stay out too late or party too much and there were times when I would do the exact opposite of what I knew I should be doing. Does any of this sound familiar?

Despite my fear that God would hold these things against me, I kept moving forward and pursuing my spirituality with the boldness and confidence that we're told to have in Hebrews 4:15-16. Just like Mary did in Luke 10:39, I came and sat right at the Lord's feet ...even with all the work that needed to be done.

In doing so, I learned a very important thing. No matter what it is we still need to work on or change about our lives, no matter what we have been told by others or how we choose to go about building our relationship with Him, God is never mad *at* us, only madly in love *with* us! I hate to think where I would be if I never realized that!

The Bible is full of scriptures that show us how much God loves and cares about us. The most important being John 3:16 (NIV), which tells us, *"For God so loved the world, that he gave his only Son, that whoever believes in him should not perish but have eternal life."* Also, Romans 5:8 (NIV) tells us, *"But God showed his love for us in that while we were still sinners, Christ died for us."*

And, in Zechariah 2:8 (NIV) Jesus tells us, *"The Glorious One has sent me against the nations that have plundered you--for whoever touches you touches the apple of His eye."*

But, even with these powerful scriptures to tell us otherwise, many people still have a hard time believing that these words apply to them. Many people walk around and feel there is something about themselves or the life they lead that causes God to say, *"I love all of my children unconditionally…well…except for maybe that one. That one right there … I'm not so sure about."*

You know how silly that sounds to read? Well, it's even sillier for us to walk around and feel!

I believe one reason people may feel this way is because they have a hard time understanding one thing …unconditional love.

In the world we live in today, almost everything comes with conditions. There are conditions when renting an apartment, buying a home or purchasing a car. You can't even buy a cell phone without a long list of conditions that, if we don't uphold, could break the agreement. All of these things come with conditions that could cause them to be taken away. However, it seems many people apply this sort of "conditional thinking" to their relationships as well.

Some people have a wish list of things they look for in a mate and oftentimes an even longer list of conditions that are "deal-breakers" that could affect the relationship.

Many marriages, friendships, and just about everything else we can think of come with terms and conditions. So, for some people, the idea of God loving and accepting us unconditionally can seem pretty far-fetched.

To think that God loves us with our less than perfect behavior, bad habits and issues and wants nothing more than to have a relationship with us and help us work on these things can be hard for some people to believe. It can seem too good to be true.

Some may think, *"You mean I can go to God with confidence and boldness and ask Him to come into my life and bless me, when I still have all of these things I need to work on?"* The answer is yes!

But, so many people have been hurt and let down by others, have been rejected and judged or have had such bad experiences in life, they start to believe things like, *"If it's too good to be true, then it usually is"* and, *"you get what you pay for."* This may be true of many things in life, but it's not true when it comes to God's love for us!

People who don't understand this often think that God's love for us is based on how well we uphold our end of the bargain.

They may think things like how well we behave, how often we go to church, how much we read the Bible or how "perfect" we try to be are the conditions of the relationship. They may believe that anytime we fall short, it affects how God feels about us.

They might think things like the type of life they lead, things they have done in the past, or mistakes they may make in the future are the "deal breakers" in our relationship with God. This can cause a person to "tip- toe" around the throne instead of coming boldly or to feel like they have to stay away from God altogether.

This reminds me of a very important story that shows how a person can end up feeling this way. It's one of the experiences that actually led me to write this book.

I have a buddy of mine who grew up with a very religious mother, who was a little overbearing with her beliefs. Even though her approach never seemed to work, she was always pestering my friend to go to church with her and asking him things like, "Are you ready to give your life over to God?"

At the time, my friend had just turned twenty-one. He was just starting out on his own and was enjoying all the fun things we experience in life at that age. He had a good job, a nice car, and his own place and was doing very well for himself. So, the thought of having to "give his life over" to anyone when he had just started living it wasn't very appealing. Not to mention, the way his mother was going about it wasn't helping much either.

Once in a while, he would go out and party, maybe drink a little too much and end up paying for it the next day, but overall, he was a good kid. I was a few years older than him and had already gone through many of the things he was experiencing, so I would often give him advice and try to keep him on the right track.

One day, after getting off the phone with his mom, he threw his phone down in disgust and said, "I'm so tired of her telling me that I'm not living right just because I like to go out, have fun and enjoy my life! Why can't we just have a normal conversation without her quoting Bible scriptures and telling me God sees everything I do? It's like she's trying to scare me. Well, if God is so upset with me, then I guess we won't have anything to do with each other. I'll just stay as far away from Him as possible!"

After having these kinds of conversations with his mom over and over, my friend had started to believe that God was mad at him because of the way he lived his life. He wasn't doing anything out of the ordinary that anyone reading this probably didn't do at that age. I knew for myself that he was a good person and came from a good family. I even understood what his mom was trying to do. But, her attempts to bring him closer to God had actually succeeded in doing the complete opposite...only scaring him further away.

Back then, I was still in the early stages of my own walk with God but I knew the critical, angry, judgmental God she was describing to him wasn't the same one I was experiencing in my own life. The God I was getting to know made me want to grow closer to Him and involve Him in everything I did, while the one my buddy was hearing about made him want to run and hide as far away as possible!

Up until this point, I had kept my relationship with God pretty much to myself. I'm a private person and my relationship with The Lord was personal.

But, this was one of the first times I felt like I had to speak up and share what I was learning. I knew that if I didn't, there was a possibility my friend would become one of those fearful, doubtful people I spoke about earlier. I could already see him start to develop the attitude of, *"Well, if God doesn't like me ...then he doesn't have to be bothered with me."*

To him, God was some angry dictator looking down from the sky always shaking His finger at him. So, of course his first instinct was to stay as far away from Him as possible. I knew that if I didn't share my perspective, he might continue to think God was "mad" at him and be too scared to ever invite Him into his life at all.

I told him many of the things I'm sharing in this chapter, even though I was just learning them myself.

I told him, "We are no secret to God. He knows every bad habit we have, every time we may drink too much or party too hard, every time we may lose our temper, have a bad attitude or fall short in any other way. He created us and knows more about us than we will ever know about ourselves, and He still loves us! So relax, you don't have to hide from God. He is not mad at you over these things."

I told him God loves us unconditionally and we are able to open up and include Him in every part of our lives, without fear. I told him we don't have to feel bad or separate ourselves from God over anything, not even our sins. I told him Jesus already paid for all the mistakes we will ever make and the closer we are to Him...the better we become!

I told him not to be afraid to ask God to come right into the middle of his life and change whatever needed to be changed. I also told him that sometimes other people will be harder on us and judge us more harshly than God ever will. I even made sure to tell him not to be mad at his mom. I told him that she only wanted the best for him and maybe this is the only way she knew how to get that across.

The way I talked to him about God must have been different than anything he had ever heard. Instead of beating him over the head with what I was learning, I tried to be a walking, talking example of what it means to have God in your life.

I still listened to the same music as he did, I still liked to go out and have fun. I was still pursuing my career in music. I still had style and liked to dress cool. I still liked to joke and be goofy. I still made mistakes and lived my life.... I just loved The Lord while doing so. And more importantly, I knew that *He* loved *me*!

I must have shown my friend a different side of God than he had ever seen. I never forced my beliefs on him but I wasn't ashamed of them either. I'm sure everyone reading this has heard that being a Christian and having God in your life is supposed to make others want some of what you have. Well, it did!

It wasn't long before I actually started to see a change in him. His attitude toward God started to turn around and he started to open up, ask questions and consider the possibility that God really wasn't "mad" at him. We would have many conversations about God and spirituality.

He would ask me things that he said he wasn't comfortable enough to ask his mom or anyone else. I saw him go from being a person who thought God didn't want anything to do with him to someone who knew God loved him and was on his side, no matter what. It was almost scary how God used me to help him see things differently!

It was also a learning experience for me as well. It was then that I realized God had a plan for me that was bigger than I even knew. I realized, even though I was still learning and growing myself, that I was able to help others. I saw how God made me more comfortable opening up, talking about my relationship with Him and sharing my perspective. I saw how that made others comfortable enough to start opening up as well.

The way I shared God with people, particularly this one friend, showed me one thing a lot more Christians could benefit from learning; you catch more flies with honey than you do with vinegar!

The more I learned, the more I shared with others around me and those conversations are much of what this book is based on.

When I talked to my friend and told him I was going to put this story in the book, he laughed. He said he couldn't believe how much he had grown since then.

He said he's still moving forward in his relationship with God and told me that his mom has even mellowed out a bit. He said now, they are able to have good conversations about God and even laugh about how pushy she used to be. But, he might not have ever reached that point if no one told him that God wasn't mad at him and loved him unconditionally. That's the first thing we *all* need to realize in order to have enough courage to move forward and experience any real victory!

It's sad to think how many people walk around every day and feel the way my friend used to. They feel like God is angry with them so they have to "hide" or keep their distance and stay as far away from Him as possible.

This is the same thing Adam and Eve did in the beginning of time, as they hid themselves from God in the Garden of Eden after Eve ate the apple. Amazingly, people are still doing the same thing today! The fear that God is mad at us keeps some people from ever coming to Him and understanding that His love for us is unconditional, no matter what.

God may not be happy with everything we say or do but that does not stop Him from loving us. God looks past what we may be at the moment and sees our potential. This can be seen in 1 Samuel 16:7 (NASB) where the Lord said to Samuel, *"Do not look at his appearance or at the height of his stature, because I have rejected him. For God sees not as man sees; man looks at the outward appearance, but the Lord looks at the heart."*

Think of it this way: some of you reading this may be parents and I'm sure you love your child unconditionally. There is nothing that you wouldn't do for him or her, but this doesn't mean you are pleased with everything that they do.

He or she may be selfish, lazy, won't listen, talk back or get in trouble in school. But, none of their bad habits takes away from the love you have for them, right? You just correct them and try to help them move through life and be better. Well, if you can feel that way about your child then why don't people think God, the ultimate parent, feels the same way about us?

Romans 3:23 (NIV), lets us know, *"For all have sinned and fallen short of the glory of God."* However, we can't let those mistakes convince us that God is angry and doesn't love us through it all. The only mistake would be to let our fear and doubt keep us away from God. To do so is pointless; God knows everything about us and still loves us anyway!

Romans 8:38-39 tells us, *"I am convinced that nothing can ever separate us from God's love. Neither death nor life, neither angels nor demons, neither our fears for today nor our worries about tomorrow—not even the powers of hell can separate us from God's love. No power in the sky above or in the earth below—indeed, nothing in all creation will ever be able to separate us from the love of God that is revealed in Christ Jesus our Lord."*

That's a pretty powerful scripture! Take a minute and just think about it; there is nothing that could ever separate us from the love of God. There is no mistake, no bad habit, no addiction, no guilt, no shame, and no circumstance that could ever cause God to stop loving us. His love is unconditional!

I want you to stop and ask yourself:

- *Have I let fear keep me away from God?*
- *Is there anything in my life that causes me to doubt how much He loves me?*
- *Am I afraid that God is angry with me in any way?*
- *Am I experiencing God's unconditional love in my life or am I running away and hiding from it?*

If the answer is running away, then it may be time to stop. You're only going to wear yourself out!

CHAPTER 3

JUST THE WAY YOU ARE!

"I praise you because I am fearfully and wonderfully made; your works are wonderful, I know that full well" (Psalm 139:14, NIV).

In the last chapter, we began talking about doubt and fear. I talked about how some people walk around each day wondering if God is mad at them over certain things in their life. I explained how feeling this way can cause a person to question whether or not God loves them and can even make them want to stay away from Him altogether. The last thing people want to do is spend time with someone they believe doesn't like them, right?

Feeling this way makes people believe they have to keep God at a distance and separate Him from other areas of their life. Believing that He is angry or unhappy with them only causes them to build that wall up higher.

These doubts and fears are what keep many people from ever coming boldly to the throne like we have been talking about, developing a relationship with God and learning to be spiritually successful.

I mentioned that there are even some people who look at letting God into their lives as a "risk". Now, I want to explain what I mean by that.

I started this book by saying, *"God created you for a reason. The things that interest you, the things you are passionate about or like to do, your talent and abilities, the dreams you have for the future, the goals you want to accomplish, none of these things are mistakes, they all have a purpose."*

I began that way because there are many people who believe that having God in your life means you will have to give up all those things. There are many people who are afraid that once you invite God in, you lose your personality and you can no longer be yourself or do some of the things you enjoy.

Earlier, I spoke about my buddy and his mother, who was always asking him if he was ready to "give his life over to God". Like my friend, there are many people who have been made to believe that having God in your life is all about what you have to "give up" and what you *can't* and *aren't* supposed to do.

There are even people who believe God wants to take away our personality, our sense of humor, our interest and talents and turn us into boring religious "robots" who go around pointing out what everyone else is doing wrong. This scares people away and couldn't be further from the truth!

Many people come to this conclusion because, let's face it… there are some believers who don't make it look like very much fun to be a Christian. And, while it's true that having God in our lives does change us, it is always for the better!

I have to admit, I used to be one of those people. I was apprehensive about letting God into my life. I was hesitant to move over and let Him take the driver's seat when I had a plan for my life that I wanted to make work. I was happy with the fact that I like to dress a certain way…in jeans, baseball hats and sneakers and not khakis and suits. I was afraid I would have to give up my love for rap music and spend the rest of my life listening to gospel if I wanted to have a relationship with God, like some people would have you believe.

I didn't realize that God made me who I am for a reason. I didn't understand that He could take all those things and use them for His glory!

There are many other people who don't realize this as well. You may even be one of them. There are many people who don't understand God created us all different for a reason and gave us all different personalities, interest, skills and talents...all which are valuable to Him.

There is no need to be afraid; God does not want to take these things away! Psalm 139:4 tells us that we are fearfully and wonderfully made and that all of God's work is marvelous. He can use any one of us to accomplish great things. But, He can only do this if we put aside our fear and let Him into our life.

In this chapter, "Just The Way You Are", I want to take a look at how God took twelve ordinary men, all with different personalities, interest, skills, strengths and weaknesses and used them to do extraordinary things. Once these men put aside their doubts and fear and decided to walk with Jesus, they went on to do great things and become some of the most important men to ever live.

Their names are Simon Peter and his brother Andrew, James and John (also brothers), Philip, Nathaniel, Matthew, Thomas, James and his brother Thaddeus, Simon and Judas...also known as The Twelve Disciples, or as I like to call them ... "Jesus's homeboys"! These men followed Jesus, learned from Him and after His crucifixion and resurrection, went on to witness and spread the gospel (all except for Judas, who betrayed Jesus, died and was replaced).

While these men were Jesus's closest companions and had an extraordinary calling on their life, they definitely had their own personalities, interest and skills, all which were important to Jesus. Among them were a few fishermen, a revolutionary and even a tax collector. I believe Jesus knew each of their different characteristics and personalities would be of use in spreading His message.

Let's take a closer look at how the twelve disciples were all different but were equally valued by Jesus.

Let's start with Peter who, at times, could be a little emotional and impulsive. Although he was very passionate and a great speaker, he could also be aggressive, which often led to him speaking out of turn and without thinking. Even still, he emerged as the best preacher out of the group.

Peter was known to swing from one extreme to another, one moment being an inspirational leader ... the next wrestling with fear and doubt.

This can be seen in Matthew 14:25- 33 (NIV), when the disciples saw Jesus walking on water.

After dismissing a huge crowd of about 5,000 people after preaching to them and feeding them all with only five loaves of bread and two fish, Jesus told the disciples to get in the boat ahead of him and go to the other side of the lake. He then went up on the mountain to pray by himself.

After staying there most of the night, He decided to meet back with the disciples shortly before dawn. Since the boat was on the other side of the lake, He walked out to them on the water.

When the disciples saw Jesus, they thought He was a ghost and were terrified. But, Jesus told them not to be afraid. Peter, full of doubt, said "Lord, if it's you, tell me to come to you on the water." Jesus told Peter to get out of the boat and come towards Him.

Peter got out of the boat, walked on the water and came towards Jesus. He was doing okay for a while, but he became distracted by the wind and the storm. Then, he got afraid and began to sink. He cried out, "Lord, save me!" Immediately, Jesus reached out His hand and caught him. *"You of little faith,"* he said, *"why did you doubt?"*

This back and forth was often the case with Peter. He had *just* witnessed Jesus feed 5,000 people with only two fish and five loaves of bread but was still unsure when Jesus told him to get out of the boat. Although he had the faith to do it, he let his doubt distract him and he began to sink.

Does this sound familiar? I know it does to me. We all wrestle with the same faith and fear mentality that Peter did in our lives from time to time. However, it didn't stop Jesus from loving Peter and valuing the good He saw in him.

Peter even let doubt get the best of him when, in Jesus's final hours, he abandoned Him and denied knowing Him not once...not twice... but three times!

Even still, Peter was dearly loved and held a special place among the twelve, often stepping up as the spokesman for the group. After the resurrection of Christ, Peter's emotion and passion led him to become a bold preacher and missionary, as well as one of the greatest and most influential leaders of the early church.

While Andrew, Peter's older brother, was eager to bring people to Christ, he was more comfortable letting Peter take the spotlight. Where Peter was the better preacher, Andrew was a great organizer and administrator. He was a logical thinker and made firm decisions. He was known among the rest of the disciples as the best judge of character and was the first to suspect trouble with Judas.

Andrew, who was originally a follower of John the Baptist, was the first follower of Jesus and responsible for leading Peter to Christ.

When John the Baptist proclaimed Jesus to be the "lamb of God" (John 1:29, NIV), Andrew went to spend some time with Him. After spending only a day with Jesus, Andrew found his brother Peter and told him, *"We have found the Messiah"* (John 1:41, NIV).

Andrew was the type of man who had to find out the truth for himself. When John the Baptist proclaimed Jesus the "lamb of God", Andrew didn't just take his word for it. Even though he was a devoted follower of John, he had to spend time with Jesus to see for himself.

As anyone reading this who has spent any amount of time in the presence of The Lord can tell you …it didn't take long for Andrew to be convinced that Jesus was the real deal! After seeing this for himself, Andrew didn't hesitate to give up his career as a fisherman and follow Jesus. He became a great missionary and then went on to preach the gospel and bring thousands into the kingdom.

Next are James and John. These two brothers, who were full of fire and enthusiasm, were nicknamed "The Sons of Thunder" by Jesus. Perhaps, it was because they had loud booming voices and larger than life personalities. Maybe they earned that nickname because, when pushed, their tempers flared up and they spoke out like a thunderous storm. Both brothers were fiercely loyal to Jesus.

Luke 9:54 (NIV), tells us that when Jesus and His disciples were traveling through Samaria on their way to Jerusalem, Jesus attempted to find a place to stay for the night but was denied by the villagers. When James and John saw this, they asked, "Lord, do you want us to call fire down from heaven to destroy them?" Jesus said *"No"*, and they simply moved on to another village. Talk about being hot tempered!

There were even instances where James and John spoke out against people who were claiming to heal people and drive out demons in Jesus's name because they were not part of the twelve disciples. Whatever the reason, these two hotheaded brothers had a fire in them that Jesus knew would serve Him well. And, even though there were times when Jesus corrected them and showed them how to go about things more smoothly, He never tried to take their passion and fire away from them.

James, the older of the two, was able to see things from all angles. He came the closest to actually understanding the great importance of their missions and got along well with the other disciples. He was courageous and only showed his temper when provoked. While John, the youngest of all the disciples could be a bit conceited, even calling himself "the disciple whom Jesus loved" but was extremely dependable and devoted.

Together, with Peter and Andrew, James and John made up Jesus's inner circle. These four men, with their unique personalities, skills, strengths and weaknesses were the closest to Jesus of all the disciples and had a front row seat for many of the miracles and amazing events that Jesus performed.

Both brothers displayed an unwavering devotion to Jesus, with James being the first to be martyred and John being the only one from the twelve at the cross during Jesus's crucifixion.

The remaining disciples were just as interesting and different. There was Philip, who was a very curious person and always had to see things to believe them. Phillip was all about the "black and white" of a situation. There were even times when he interrupted Jesus in mid-sermon to ask questions! Philip was very matter-of-fact and mathematical. Some might even say that he lacked imagination.

Because of his thorough and systematic nature, he was given the job of steward. It was his duty to see that Jesus and the disciples always had supplies and provisions.

Jesus put Philip's practicality to the test during the feeding of 5,000 people. Jesus asked him how they could buy bread for such a huge crowd. Philip immediately started calculating and said that even eight months of wages would not be enough for each person to get one bite.

Can you imagine how amazed Philip must have been to see Jesus feed the enormous crowd with only two fish and five loaves of bread? It is said that Philip was also one of the disciples present at Jesus's first miracle …turning water into wine. Even though Philip did not fully understand everything that was happening, he accepted it because he recognized Jesus as the Messiah. Even though he was not a great public speaker, after Jesus's resurrection, Philip continued to do evangelistic work and win souls for the kingdom.

The sixth disciple, Nathaniel, was a very honest and sincere person but could also be prideful and quick to judge. It is said in John 1:46 (ESV), that before he even met Jesus he immediately asked the question, *"Can anything good come out of Nazareth?"* However, he was equally as quick to take it back once he looked into Jesus's face.

He also had a great sense of humor, was the best storyteller out of the group and never took himself too seriously. Jesus really enjoyed hearing Nathaniel's opinion on everything from the serious to the humorous. These characteristics even caused Judas to go to Jesus in secret and complain that Nathaniel didn't take his responsibilities as a disciple seriously enough.

When Judas did this, Jesus replied, *"Judas watch carefully your steps, do not over magnify your office. Who of us is competent to judge his brother? It is not the Fathers will that His children should partake in only the serious things in life. I have come so my brethren in the flesh may have joy, gladness and life more abundantly. Go then Judas and do that which has been entrusted to you, but leave Nathaniel, your brother, to give an account of himself."*

In other words, Jesus told Judas to mind his own business!

Many times, if things became tense while Jesus was away on the mountain, Nathaniel would often lift everyone's spirits with his humor. He was also given the responsibility to look after the families of the other disciples. It was a responsibility he took with great pride, so he was often absent from the gatherings.

Little is known about what happened to Nathaniel after Jesus's resurrection. The other disciples were left to wonder what became of him. However, it is believed that he continued to spread Jesus's teachings and baptize believers throughout Mesopotamia and India.

The seventh disciple, Matthew, belonged to a family of tax collectors. Matthew was a great businessman, good in social situations and had the ability to make friends with a variety of people. These characteristics made him a great politician and therefore he became responsible for raising money for Jesus's cause. The other disciples often referred to him as the "money –getter". I'm sure we could all use someone with that quality around!

However, it did take some time for the other disciples to warm up to the idea of having a tax collector among them. At times, Matthew could be materialistic and short sighted. But, he grew to believe in, what he called, the "business of finding God". He believed in Jesus's mission so wholeheartedly, that he often funded the disciple's cause straight from his own pocket. The only one who knew about this was Jesus. All the disciples died without knowing Matthew was the source of much of their money. Still, they all were proud of his growth and performance. After persecution caused the believers to leave Jerusalem, Matthew went on to journey forward and preach the gospel and baptize thousands of people.

Next, there was Thomas, who had a very logical and sometimes skeptical way of thinking, (this is where we get the term "doubting Thomas"). Even though Thomas had unflinching courage and a very sharp and reasoning mind, he was also a natural faultfinder and could be very pessimistic. It took many of the other disciples, especially Peter, time to really get to know Thomas and like him, despite his suspicious nature. Thomas even went through bouts of depression and would go off alone for a day or two. He soon realized that it was best to stay with the group and was helped through these times by the other disciples and his relationship with Jesus.

If Jesus and His work were not genuine, He could have never convinced someone like Thomas to follow Him. But, despite his moods and doubting suspicions, Jesus enjoyed Thomas very much. This goes to show that Jesus even loves those who may doubt Him!

The fact that Thomas was a disciple actually drew many unbelievers into the Kingdom. Even if they didn't fully understand the teachings of Jesus, they figured if a man like Thomas could believe...then so could they!

Thomas was a good businessman and was given the job to manage the itinerary. After Jesus's crucifixion, Thomas sunk into a deep depression. However, he gathered his strength, stuck with the rest of the disciples and was there to welcome Jesus after His resurrection. He then went on to preach the gospel, baptize believers and bring many people into the kingdom.

Another set of brothers, James and Thaddeus Alpheus understood very little about the debates that went on among their fellow disciples. Nevertheless, they were just happy to be included among such great men. Even though they are sometimes referred to as "the lesser apostles", they were always willing and eager to help out wherever they were needed.

They often helped Philip with supplies, took things to the other disciple's families for Nathaniel and were even given the duty of policing the crowds when it was time for Jesus to preach. Some say the crowds were more than willing to listen to James and Thaddeus because they didn't mind being directed by regular people who were just like themselves.

Even though these brothers might have been looked at as being simple, they were kind, generous and everyone loved them. Their simple existence might have even helped to draw others into the Kingdom because it showed people that Jesus looked down on no one.

Soon after Jesus was crucified, they returned home but were changed forever by their four years of close and personal work with Jesus.

The disciple Simon was often referred to as "Simon the Zealot", because of his fiery passion as a revolutionary. Even though he often spoke without thinking, Simon was often the one called upon when the disciples ran across someone who was on the fence about joining Jesus and His cause. It usually took only about fifteen minutes of listening to Simon before they were ready to commit!

Simon was a natural rebel and a great debater. He often had many talks with Jesus about the advancement of social, economic and political issues versus the advancement of the spirit. Even though some of Jesus's teachings were difficult for him to grasp at first, Simon went on to become a powerful and effective preacher. After the disciples left Jerusalem, Simon went on to preach the message of Jesus and baptize believers throughout Africa.

Lastly, there was Judas, who is famous for betraying Jesus for thirty pieces of silver. While on the outside Judas appeared to be the perfect disciple, organized, good with money, educated, and highly respected by the others, some say Jesus knew the dangers of admitting him into the ranks. It is said that while Judas may have believed in Jesus, he never truly loved Him like the other disciples did. Jesus still gave Judas an opportunity because He believed everyone deserved an equal chance for salvation.

While Judas learned the teachings of Jesus, he never grew enough spiritually to put them to use. I'm sure everyone reading this knows someone like that, a person who can quote the Bible backwards and forward...but rarely puts any of it to use.

John 12:6 (NLT), tells us that Judas was a thief and even stole from the disciple's moneybag during his time as treasurer.

Jesus warned Judas many times that he was slipping and did everything possible to prevent Judas from choosing the wrong path. Slowly, over time Judas began to resent Jesus and become distrustful of the other disciples. His heart began to harbor hate, malice, jealousy and he yearned for revenge.

Even though during his trial, many of the disciples, (except John) left Jesus and Peter even denied knowing Him, Judas went much further. He led the guards to Jesus and betrayed Him with a kiss.

Judas experienced brief moments of shame and regret over what he had done and hoped Jesus would use His own power to deliver Himself. When that didn't happen, Judas committed the final act in his shameful story- his own suicide.

The other disciples, however, went on to do great things and become some of the most important men in the Bible.

Taking a closer look at the twelve disciples shows how much Jesus valued each one of them. We see how He was able to use their different personalities, skills, interest and talents to accomplish great things. It didn't matter where they were from or even about their particular weaknesses. All that mattered is that they made the choice to put aside their doubts and fear and follow Him. Each one of them had something unique and different to offer and guess what... so do we!

Looking at how Jesus accepted each one of these men shows us that God doesn't want to take away from who we are. He only wants to add to it, make us better and help us accomplish great things.

For example, seeing how Jesus was able to use all of the disciples differently, helped me realize that I didn't have to give up the way I like to dress, the type of music I listen to or lose my personality in order for God to use me. The same goes for you!

This brings up something that happened recently where God showed me how valuable those things really are to Him.

I was in the barbershop getting my hair cut. My barber and I always discuss books, so I was telling him about what I was working on. We started talking about God and spirituality. I was telling him some of the things I was writing about in this book.

Before I knew it, a crowd had gathered around and was listening to our conversation. The guy sitting next to us even took off his headphones and began asking questions. Soon, the whole barbershop had joined in the conversation. People were asking questions about God, the book I was writing and spirituality...all while dressed in our jeans, t-shirts and chilling with rap music playing in the background.

Many of them said they had questions that were on their mind but they just hadn't found the right person to ask. Some said they would have felt judged or looked down upon by some people who call themselves "Christians" ...so they had just been keeping those questions to themselves.

It was an awesome feeling to be the person God used to open up that type of dialogue and make people feel comfortable. It showed me the things some people say you need to change about yourself are the very *same* things God can use to help change others!

Much like the crowds were with James and Thaddeus Alpheus, people are comfortable with people who are like themselves. You never know who you may be able to help or what God may be able to do with you, "Just The Way You Are"!

Just look at the disciples. Jesus was able to use Peter's boldness, Andrew's organization, James and John's fire and passion, Philip's curiosity, Nathaniel's humor, Matthew's business mind, Simon's inspiration …and even Thomas's doubt. We never know what God can use about us and in what way.

My favorite preacher, Joyce Meyer, says she always wonders why God gave her such a loud, booming voice and "tell it like it is" personality. Even though she spent years trying to change those things and become more like the quiet, modest women in her church, it is those things that attract people to her now worldwide ministry!

On the other hand, you have people like Pastor Joel Osteen, who is more laid back and reserved but commands an audience of thousands every week in his Houston, Texas mega church. There are also people like Tyler Perry, who may not be a preacher, but teaches many lessons about God, forgiveness and being a good Christian through comedy with his plays and movies.

There are singers like Mary J. Blige, Jill Scott and rappers like Jay-Z, Kendrick Lamar and J.Cole who help others with messages about life through their music. And yet still, people like Oprah Winfrey who has been touching an audience of millions for years with her spirituality and generosity.

You never know what qualities God is able to use, if you only give Him a chance. So, take a moment and ask yourself:

- *What is unique and different about me that God can put to good use if I let Him?*
- *What skills and talents do I possess that God can use to elevate me to greatness, if I put aside my doubts and fear and walk with Him?*

Some people will never find out because they are afraid God wants to take those things away. Don't continue to let that fear stop you from inviting Him into your life. Doing so will only make you miss out on your destiny and all the great things He has for you.

God created you to be "Just The Way You Are" ...so don't be afraid to give Him a chance to show you what He can do with it!

SECTION 2

COMMUNICATING WITH GOD

CHAPTER 4

GET TO KNOW GOD

"But, from there you will seek the Lord your God, and you will find Him, if you look for Him with all your heart and soul" (Deuteronomy 4:29, NASB).

After reading the first few chapters, hopefully, some people will have a better understanding of how much God really loves us. Understanding some of the things we have been talking about so far certainly helped me open up to the possibility of having God in my own life.

Once I realized that we don't have to try and earn God's love, that He loves us unconditionally and that He doesn't want to take away any of the good things that make us who we are, I was eager to move forward in my relationship with Him. But, then I was faced with the question of, *"What next?"*

I knew that I didn't have any interest in learning by going to church and wanted to develop my relationship with God in my own way, so I had to ask myself:

- *How do I do that?*
- *How do I pray and what should I say when I do?*
- *How do I hear from God?*
- *What should I look for?*
- *Does He speak in a loud booming voice accompanied by lightning and thunder?*

- *Are there trumpets and angels signaling His arrival when He speaks to us?*
- *How do I know it's really Him?*

It may seem silly but some of you reading this may have some of the same questions and that's okay! Some people spend their entire lives in church and still wonder some of these exact things.

In this chapter, "Get to Know God", I'll begin sharing some important things I have learned about building a close, personal relationship with The Lord. We'll take a look at some of the things that are required on *our* part to have type of relationship with Him that goes beyond just memorizing Bible verses and sitting in church on Sunday.

Each one of us has the opportunity to have a close and powerful relationship with God. So, why do some people seem more "in tune" with The Holy Spirit than others?

Is it because they go to church more often? Maybe. But, there are many Christians who go to church every Sunday who still don't have a strong connection to God.

Does God give special access to some people and not others? No, we are all His children and what is available to one of us is available to all of us, (Acts 10:34).

So, what's the reason some people are closer to Him than others?

Let's start by looking at Deuteronomy 4:29, which says, *"But, from there you will seek the Lord your God, and you will find Him, if you look for Him with all your heart and soul."*

To pursue something with all your heart and soul means you want it above all else. There are many people who go after what they want in life with all their heart and soul. But, many times, those things tend to be along the lines of cars, homes, a career, fame, fortune, and love. How many people do you know who are pursuing a relationship with God with the same passion? Probably not many.

In other words, many people will never have the type of connection they want with God because they don't go after a relationship with Him with the same excitement, passion and determination that they do other things in their life.

There is nothing wrong with chasing after the things you want in life. I'm a strong believer in setting goals and making them happen. But, Matthew 6:33 (KJV) tells us, *"Seek ye first the kingdom of God, and His righteousness; and all these things shall be added unto you."*

If more people made it a priority to get to know God, they may find they don't have to chase after the things they want in life because those things would chase after them!

But, many people never make the commitment to put God first. Even many Christians make this mistake by not spending much time outside of church getting to know the Holy Spirit.

Think of it this way: if someone told you that you were going to meet your favorite celebrity, I'm sure you would be excited. You may have seen all of their movies, bought their music, read about them online, follow them on social media or even joined their fan club.

Even though you know many things about this person, you would still have to spend time developing a relationship with them to *really* get to know who they are. No matter how much information you had about them, it could never replace the time you spend getting to know them for yourself.

Well, it's the same with God! Many people join His "fan club" but never really get to know who He is!

Some people let the sort of things we have been talking about so far (feeling unapproved, thinking God is "mad" at them or believing that He wants to turn them into some sort of boring "religious person") scare them away from taking the time to get to know Him.

Others don't feel like they can develop a relationship with Him because they don't go to church. Yet, some people who attend church every Sunday *still* don't develop a real relationship with God because they think just being in the building is enough.

In Matthew 7:21- 23, Jesus tells us that without *knowing* God and having a personal relationship with Him, it doesn't matter how many things we claim to do in His name.

The passage reads: *"Not everyone who says to me, 'Lord, Lord,' will enter the kingdom of Heaven, but the one who does the will of my Father who is in heaven. On that day many will say to me, 'Lord, Lord, did we not prophesy in your name, and cast out demons in your name, and do many mighty works in your name?' And then I will declare to them, 'I never knew you; depart from me, you workers of lawlessness"* (ESV).

I don't want anyone reading this to miss out on their opportunity to get to know God and be one of those people! Each of us already has everything we need inside us to start developing a *real* relationship with Him right now.

Aside from making it a priority to develop our relationship with God, another thing we must do in order to get to know Him is to get to know His Word. You can choose to do this in whatever way suits you best. One of the unique things about my journey is that I chose not to develop my spirituality by going to church.

I knew from the times that I did go to church when I was younger, that it wasn't for me. As I said in the introduction to this book, I don't like to wake up early, dress up or socialize with a lot of people. I would spend the entire time making funny faces at the girls from my class who sang in the choir, fidgeting in the uncomfortable clothes I was wearing and thinking about what was for dinner when I got out.

During my teenage years, my mom was exploring her own spirituality and we went to all kinds of churches. We went to churches that were so uptight, the people would look at you funny if you let out an "Amen". We went to churches where, at the end of the service, my mom and I were the only two people left sitting upright in our chairs. Everyone else had caught the "Holy ghost", ran around the church and fallen out on the floor. Despite going to different types of churches and listening to different preachers, nothing seemed to fit.

Besides being very entertaining, all those experiences served one purpose. They showed me that if I was going to get to know God, it would have to be in the way that was right for *me*.

When I was fifteen, my mom asked me to go to church with her on Mother's Day. When we walked out, after an hour and a half, I remember telling her, "Mom, I got absolutely nothing out of that."

She looked at me and said, "Well, I did what I was supposed to when you were younger and took you to church. If you know that doesn't work for you, you have to find out what does."

That was the last time I stepped foot inside a church.

What I did discover that worked for me is finding a great teacher on television, Joyce Meyer. It was through listening to her teachings over the years that I learned the Word of God and how to go about developing a relationship with Him.

I found that waking up every morning, tuning into her program, "Life in the Word" (it's now called "Enjoying Everyday Life"), listening to her teaching cd's, watching her on YouTube, becoming a partner in her ministry and even attending conferences when she came to the area worked better for me than trying to sit in church every Sunday.

Her humorous, no-nonsense, practical approach to spirituality kept me entertained. The convenience of popping in a teaching cd while driving, getting dressed or working out helped me take God out of the "Sunday morning box" and do exactly what her ministry set out to do, which was show me how to involve Him in my everyday life.

The time I spent learning God's Word helped me involve Him in everything I did. It allowed me to really get to know Him and helped build the relationship I have with Him today. I hope one day she is able to read this and see how her ministry has influenced others to step out and pass on what they have learned from her. She is truly awesome.

Much of that story and the point of this chapter is this; you have to do what is right for you. You will never be able to move forward and develop your relationship with God if you don't find the method that works best for you in getting to know Him.

I mentioned earlier in the book that people learn in different ways. Some people have to write things down, others have to read them over and over, while some only have to hear them once.

Since we all learn in many different ways, why wouldn't the same thing apply when learning about God and His Word?

Some people like to wake up early, dress nice and go to church to fellowship with others. Some people, like me, are more private and work better on their own. It was easier for me to just study, do the work and then pass on what I learned in a different way…like writing a book. When developing your relationship with God, there is no right or wrong. There is only what's right and wrong *for you.*

In Matthew 18:20 (ESV), The Lord says, *"For where two or three gather in my name, there I am with them."*

In the past, church may have been the only place that was happening. Today, there are many ways to learn God's Word, get to know Him and develop your spirituality.

There are many great preachers like Joyce Meyer, Creflo Dollar, Joel Osteen, Benny Hinn, John Hagee and T.D Jakes who have websites, books, television programs, teaching cd's and DVD's. There are even movies like the mini-series *The Bible*, which attracted millions of viewers and is available on DVD and Blu-Ray. I'm sure *The Bible*, with it's intense action sequences and suspenseful storytelling sparked many conversations and attracted the attention of people who may or may not have ever stepped foot inside a church.

Some of the best conversations I have had about God have been with friends who have seen me with a Joyce Meyer book and asked me about it. Those conversations have led to me passing along teaching cd's, books, and DVD's to them. A few have even gone to conferences with me when she came to town. When it comes to getting to know God, there's no set blueprint on how it has to be done.

If you are attending a good church on a regular basis and it works for you, that's great! But, there are many people who go to church who aren't growing spiritually and go just because they think it's the only way to get to know God.

The only way to *really* get to know God is through Jesus Christ and the last time I checked… He wasn't confined to four walls and a building!

God's Word is readily available and no time is that more evident than it is now. Technology is ever expanding and therefore so is our access to God and His Word.

We can look things up on the Internet, watch YouTube videos and download Bible apps on our phones, (some of them will even read themselves out loud).

We just have to do what the scripture says in Deuteronomy 4:29 (NASB) and *seek* The Lord. Remember, *seek* is an action word. It requires effort on our part. It may take some time to find out what works for you. But, once you do, if you go after it with *all* your heart and soul, you *will* find Him like the scripture says!

If one thing doesn't work for you, try another. I hate to think where I would be right now if I had just given up on getting to know God because going to church didn't work for me. I probably would not have grown spiritually, have the relationship with God I have now or be able to pass any of it along.

My experience hasn't been any less valuable because it hasn't taken place inside the walls of a church and yours doesn't have to be either! Whatever method you choose, start getting to know God today.

If you stay focused and determined to go after that relationship with the same passion you do other things in life, you won't be disappointed!

Pretty soon, when people start to notice a change in you and ask, "Where do you go to church?" you can look at them and say the same thing I do: "I don't go to church… the church goes with me!"

CHAPTER 5

COME AND TALK TO ME

"Rejoice always, pray without ceasing, give thanks in all circumstances; for this is the will of God in Christ Jesus for you" (1 Thessalonians 5:16-18, ESV).

Now that you know how important it is to take time to get to know God, you can work on figuring out the way that works best for you. It doesn't always happen by going to church on Sunday and that's okay!

In the world we live in today, there are many ways to study the Word of God. Nowadays, by just logging onto Facebook or Instagram, you can be encouraged, inspired and exposed to the Word of God. In our technology driven society, you can even find Jesus on social media!

Once you find out what works best for you, you can get into a groove and actually begin *enjoying* the learning process. But, while learning about God and His Word is a great first step in getting to know Him... it's only the beginning.

There are countless Christians who have read the Bible cover to cover and can recite scriptures backwards and forward, but don't have any real connection to the Holy Spirit. This is because they have never moved past the first step!

This is what I meant in the last chapter by saying; *"Many people join God's 'fan club', but never get to know Him."*

Well, *"How else can I get to know Him?"* you might ask. A great way to get to know God and develop a close relationship with Him is through one of the most powerful tools available to us... prayer.

There are many scriptures in the Bible that tell us how powerful prayer is.

In 2 Chronicles 7:14 (NIV), the Lord appeared to Solomon and said, *"If my people, which are called by my name, shall humble themselves, and pray, and seek my face, and turn from their wicked ways; then I will hear from Heaven and will forgive their sin, and will heal their land."* (See, there's that word *"seek"* again!)

James 5:14-15 (KJV) says, *"Is any sick among you? Let him call for the elders of the church; and let them pray over him, anointing him with oil in the name of the Lord: And the prayer of faith shall save the sick, and the Lord shall raise him up; and if he have committed sins, they shall be forgiven him."*

And, Mark 11:24 (NIV) says, *"Therefore I tell you, whatever you ask for in prayer, believe that you have received it, and it will be yours."*

Prayer is our direct line to God. Through our prayers, we are able grow closer to Him and strengthen that relationship.

Some people may think, *"But isn't prayer only for asking God for what we want and making our needs known to Him?"* Absolutely not!

Of course, being able to ask God for things we want and need is a benefit of prayer but it shouldn't be the only reason we do it.

Think about it this way: I'm sure there are a few of you reading this who spend a good part of your day with a cell phone glued to your ear or in your hand texting. The whole time you are communicating with friends, you aren't asking them for favors or telling them what you want or what you need. If you did, I'm sure it wouldn't be long before some of them stopped answering your calls!

You probably spend time on the phone with friends talking about *many* different things. You might talk about your dreams, goals, something you saw that was funny, a situation or person that is aggravating you, a change you're trying to make in your life or any number of things you feel comfortable discussing with a friend. Well, it should be the same way when we talk to God!

We can use our prayers to give thanks, praise, ask questions, talk about our feelings or to just "check in" throughout the day. We are able to use prayer as a *constant flow* of communication between ourselves and God. When you think about it like that, it's pretty awesome.

Some of you may be thinking, *"You mean I can talk to God about everything that's going on in my life?"* The answer is "Yes!"

Philippians 4:6 -7 (NLT) tells us, *"Don't worry about anything; instead, pray about everything. Tell God what you need, and thank him for all he has done. If you do this, you will experience God's peace, which is far more wonderful than the human mind can understand. His peace will guard your hearts and minds as you live in Christ Jesus."*

In this chapter, "Come and Talk to Me", I will continue to talk about getting to know God on a deeper level. This time, we will focus on how we can develop a close and powerful relationship with Him through prayer. I'll help you learn how to not just communicate with God about the "spiritual" or "Holy" things in your life…but about everything!

Everywhere we look, people seem to be in need of *someone* to tell their feelings to. Whether it's on talk shows, social media or that co-worker who talks your ear off…people just want someone who will *listen*. Well, look no further; we all have someone who is willing and eager to hear from us. And, I guarantee you, His response will be more powerful than a "Like" or a "Thumbs Up"!

One thing you will discover while studying the Word of God is how much God really wants to have a relationship with each one of His children. Jeremiah 24:7 (NIV) states, *"I will give them a heart to know me, that I am the Lord. They will be my people, and I will be their God, for they will return to me with all their heart."* Psalm 149:4 tells us, *"The Lord takes pleasure in His people"*, and Isaiah 62:4 says that The Lord "delights" in us.

God wants to have a close relationship with us and is concerned with every aspect of our lives. This means we are able to open up and talk to Him about everything going on with us. If we are concerned about it, then so is God!

God is concerned with our:

- ❖ Finances
- ❖ Family and Social Life

- ❖ Health
- ❖ Dreams and Goals
- ❖ Our Issues and Problems
- ❖ The Things We Like to Do

All of these things are important to Him. So, we should feel free to talk to Him about these things when we pray. But, there are many people who don't.

Many people think praying is reserved for only the "big" things in their lives. These people make the mistake of only reaching out to God when things in their life get serious and they need Him the most. They may not understand that God wants to be a part of our lives *every day*, whether we have some big "need" or not.

This is one reason some people aren't as close to God as they would like to be. You can't have a close relationship with God, (or anyone else for that matter), if you shut them out and only reach out when you need them for something.

There are also those who believe prayer and communicating with God has to be a long, difficult process. These are the people who think you have to use big words and speak to God as if we were still living in Biblical times. This can intimidate people and scare them off to the point where they don't even try to pray.

One of the first things I learned about how to pray and communicate with God is how simple the process really is. Matthew 6:7-8 (ESV) tells us, *"When you pray, do not heap up empty phrases as the Gentiles do, for they think that they will be heard for their many words. Do not be like them, for your Father knows what you need before you ask Him."*

Also, Mark 10:15 (NLT) says, *"I tell you the truth, anyone who doesn't receive the kingdom of God like a little child will never enter it."* These scriptures helped me a lot as I started to develop my relationship with God through prayer.

Think about how little children look at the world. They are fun loving, full of hope, positivity and laughter. They are light hearted and don't seem to have a care in the world.

When they talk to their parents, they don't sit around wondering what to say and how to say it. They just say it!

I'm sure everyone reading this has been somewhere in public when a child has been talking to their parent, non –stop. They tell them about everything from what happened in school that day to the latest video game.

Some of them are so excited that they don't even pause to take a breath! In other words, they don't over - think the process.

Well, God wants us to be the same way with Him! God wants us to be just as excited talk to Him about our lives as those little kids are with their parents. He wants us to feel free to come to Him anytime and about anything…without worrying about what to say and how to say it.

Trust me, God is much more pleased by the time we decide to spend with Him than the production we put on when we do!

But, there are still reasons why people don't feel they can open up and talk to God this way.

Some people feel guilty about some of the things that are going on in their lives and therefore don't feel like they can talk to God about them. Some people have been so hurt, looked down upon and judged by others, they feel God won't care either… so why bother talking to Him?

Even worse, some people don't even realize that they *can* have this type of close relationship with God despite some of those things. Even some Christians make this mistake when they believe the only connection they have to God is through whoever they may be learning from, which couldn't be further from the truth!

In many instances, people run to the pastor of the church for advice and counseling, which is perfectly fine. Everyone needs encouragement and guidance from the right people. But, don't make the mistake of letting this take the place of going to God and talking to Him for *yourself*!

Whatever the case, God wants us to open up and feel comfortable talking to Him no matter what the situation.

He doesn't want us to feel as though we have to change in any way before we begin to talk to Him. He doesn't want us to feel as though we have to hide ourselves or any part of our lives from Him. He knows the truth anyway. He is *God* after all!

Talk to God like you would talk to a friend. It doesn't have to be a long process full of big words. After all, we've already learned that God approves, accepts and created us to be just who we are. And, *that's* the person He wants to hear from!

Once you are comfortable enough to open the lines of communication between yourself and God, you'll find a way to move forward that feels right for you. Some people have a certain time of day that they pray and talk to God, some have a quiet place that they like to go, while others do so all throughout the day.

Thessalonians 5:17 tells us to "pray without ceasing", and as I learned to communicate with God, that's just what I did. Not only did I keep the lines of prayer and thanksgiving open 24/7, but the lines of communication, period. I talked to God anywhere and anytime, about everything. I talked to Him about my insecurities, fears, dreams, hopes, interest, things I found funny, and even my sins and shortcomings.

In addition to praying about the big things in my life, I learned to include Him in the little things as well. There have been times when I have prayed before going out with friends. I would ask God to let us have a good time, show balance and self-control by not drinking too much and arrive home safely.

I have prayed before performances for everything to go right with the sound and microphones, to have favor with the crowds and especially to remember my lyrics!

I have even prayed before going to the mall, not to overspend, find great deals and get a good parking space. In other words, I learned to involve God in everything I did. This is how I grew close to Him!

This may sound silly to some of you, but how can you expect God to bless every area of your life…if you don't open up and include Him in every area of your life?

I want you to know; this type of close and powerful relationship with God through prayer is available to each and every one of you. Psalm 145: 18 (ISV) says, *"The Lord remains near to all who call out to him, to all who call out to him sincerely."*

Everything you need to start developing this type of relationship with God is already inside of you. You just have to open up and let Him in. So, take the first step and drop Him a line… I'm sure He'll be glad to hear from you!

CHAPTER 6

WATCH, HOPE AND EXPECT

"He made from one blood all nations who live on the earth. He set the times and places where they should live. They were to look for God. Then they might feel after Him and find Him because He is not far from each one of us" (Acts 17:26-27, NLV).

After hearing about the awesome all-access pass we have to God through prayer, I hope you will use it often. I encourage you to pray and talk to God, not only about the big things in life, but the little things as well.

Communication is a huge part of any relationship and the more we communicate with someone, the closer we become. It's the same way with God! The more we make an effort to include Him in every part of our lives, the stronger our relationship with Him will be.

But, as anyone who has read any sort of book on relationships or has seen at least one talk show will tell you; communication is a two way street. So, here comes the exciting part!

By opening up the lines of communication between ourselves and God, we throw the door wide open for Him to communicate back with us! But, what does that really mean?

I'm sure everyone reading this has heard someone say, "God spoke to me and said..." or "I got a 'word' from God that told me what to do."

Does it mean that angels showed up, trumpets blared and lightening lit up the sky? Probably not.

God is probably not going to physically manifest, tap you on the shoulder and say, *"Hey, this is what you should do."* But, He will often communicate and "speak" to us through things in our everyday life. He is very creative!

Things we are interested in, people we may come into contact with, a feeling in our gut or almost anything else in our lives can become an opportunity for God to communicate with us.

This is one reason why it is so important to have a close relationship with God. You want to be able to recognize it when He tries to get through to you. It can make life much easier!

Once we learn how to become in tune with the "voice" of the Holy Spirit, we will truly see that we are *not* alone, God is *real*, He hears us, and is *always* on our side! But, in order to have this type of connection with Him and experience life this way, we have to understand a few important things.

In this chapter, "Watch, Hope and Expect", I want to talk about how we can become better at hearing the "voice" of God. I'll share some tips on how to recognize God's attempts to communicate with us, answer our questions and help us in our everyday life. I will talk about why it is easy for some people to do this and harder for others. We'll also take a look at the mistakes some people make that cause them to "miss" God when He tries to get through to them.

Let's start by taking a look at Job 33:14, which says, *"For God speaks in one way, and in two, though man does not perceive it"* (ESV).

To me, this scripture says God may try to get through to us in one way, He may even try a couple different things, but many times we don't perceive it. Why is that?

I believe one reason people may not see God when He shows up in their life is because ...they aren't looking for Him! It seems simple, but it's true. It's much easier to find something when you're looking for it, right?

Jeremiah 29:13 (NIV) tell us, *"You will seek me and find me when you seek me with all your heart."*

We've already talked about how "seek" is a verb and requires action on our part. Jeremiah 29:13 tells us to *seek* God with all our heart and we will find Him. It doesn't say, *"Walk through life never looking for God around you and then wonder why you can't hear from Him!"*

One reason many people have trouble seeing God around them is because they won't do one simple thing ... slow down. I can tell you this; you'll never find Him if you don't slow down and look for Him!

In the world we live in today, people are so consumed by the hectic pace of everyday life, that they often miss it when God tries to speak to them. People are so busy working, raising children, paying bills, going to school, trying to accomplish their goals, having a social life and yes, even so busy going to church, that they often rush right by God and all the ways He may be trying to get their attention and communicate with them.

In a documentary about her life, Oprah Winfrey said that the "universe" (her way of saying God), first speaks to us in whispers. This is very true!

Many times, the answers to the problems and questions we have are right in front of our face, but we are moving so fast that we don't see them.

For example, I remember one day I was rushing around trying to get out of the house while talking on my cell phone at the same time. I grabbed my keys and wallet, but it seemed like I was forgetting something. I couldn't seem to put my finger on what it was. I was so busy running around trying to figure out what I was missing, I didn't realize that I had spent a few minutes in a mad rush looking for my cell phone, which was in my hand.

I was moving so fast that I didn't realize what I was searching for was right there!

This is how people often miss God. They move so fast that they miss the little things, the obvious, the "whispers" that are all around us. Oftentimes, this is God trying to get our attention and communicate with us.

I like to think of it as God standing on the side of the highway of our lives waving a big orange flag, saying, *"Hey, here I am!" "Look over here!"* How many times are we moving so fast that we speed right by

Him and don't see all the ways He tries to communicate with us, simply because we won't slow down and take the time to look for them?

The more we slow down, the more we will start to recognize all the ways, big or small, that God is around us.

Some of you may be thinking, *"Well, once I slow down...what next? What do I look for?"* The short answer is… everything!

Psalms 5:3 tells us that each morning we should bring our requests to The Lord and wait expectantly. The word "expectantly" is very important here. It means, *"the state of thinking or hoping that something, especially something pleasant, will happen"* (1913 Webster).

This scripture tells us that we should make our request known to God and *expect* Him to get back to us.

Micah 7:7 (NIV) states, *"But as for me, I watch in hope for the Lord, I wait for God my Savior; my God will hear me."* The most important words in that scripture are "watch" and "hope". Both of these scriptures emphasize how important it is for us to not only wait on God, but to wait *expectantly* ... watching and hoping for Him to show up in our lives at any moment!

Once we learn how to "Watch, Hope and Expect" God to show up in our lives, we will start to realize how much He really does.

We seem to have no problem waiting expectantly on other people. How many times have you invited someone over to your house and around the time they were supposed to arrive, you looked out the window, listened out for a knock at the door or checked your cellphone? You had your eyes and ears open because you were *expecting* them to show up. Well, we need to learn to do the same for God.

How many of you reading this have people in your lives that you consider to be very dependable? If you need them and call them, they will come. If your car breaks down and you are stranded on the highway, you can call them and *expect* them to show up. You don't have to spend your time worrying if they will show up or wondering if they understood how bad you needed help.

Well, if we are able to put this much faith in another person to expect them show up in our lives when we need them, why can't we do the same with God? He is much more dependable than people!

If we learn to wait upon Him and watch for Him in our lives with expectancy and hope, it makes living our everyday lives much more exciting because we never know when or how He is going to show up with answers!

My favorite R&B singer, Jill Scott, says, *"God is ever present. He's in every breath, in every step. He's here.... always."*

This is how I learned to look at life. I learned to live every moment of every day watching for God around me and expecting Him to show up like it says to do in Psalms 5:3. And, just like it says in Jeremiah 29:13, we will find Him when we seek Him with all our heart.

These two scriptures were very powerful in helping me learn to recognize God when He tried to communicate with me.

For example, if I was worried about a certain problem or situation in my life and saw a sign for car insurance while driving down the interstate that read, *"Don't worry.... I got you covered!"* or an advertisement for a gas station that said, *"What you need is right around the corner"*, then I would look at that as a reassuring sign from God!

I mean, how else do we expect to find Him…if we don't start paying attention to the things around us?

This reminds me of something that happened recently that shows how God can use something that is *literally* right in front of us to communicate with us. While writing this book, I was faced with many doubts. I had never written a book before. I knew nothing about publishing, literary agents, book proposals or marketing. I had to step out on faith and learn as I went. I put my music on hold to focus on writing this book and basically put all my eggs in one basket…without knowing if it would even work.

One day, as I was driving…those doubts began to overwhelm me. As I felt myself begin to stress out and sink into double mindedness, I prayed. I asked God to send me a sign that I was doing the right thing and that all my hard work wasn't going to be in vain.

Almost immediately, I snapped back to reality and looked at the car that had been driving in front of me the whole time. The first three letters of the license plate were "RMX" …the abbreviation for "Remix"! Now, I could have chosen to ignore that, take it as coincidence or not think anything of it at all and continue to worry. However, why would I pray to God for a sign that writing this book was the right thing to do, suddenly notice a word from the title of the book almost spelled out on the car right in front of me and ignore that?

Some of you may be thinking, *"Well, those are just ordinary things that people see everyday, why would God use them to speak to you?"* The answer is …because I am looking for Him!

Granted, the answers may not be as immediate as that example but they'll really be delayed if you never start looking!

I learned to put on, what I like to call, my "God Glasses" and began to look for Him everywhere. As I began to "Watch, Hope and Expect" God to show up, I saw that He can use literally *anything* in our lives to communicate with us. To this day, I'm still amazed at all the ways He chooses to show up and make Himself known!

I have always loved music, so God has often chosen to speak to me this way. It can be a lyric from a song I can't seem to get out of my head, something an artist may say in an interview, a line from a movie, or a million other things that can make the light bulb go off above my head.

For example, this reminds me of a time where God used a song to speak to me when I was going through something.

As I may mention several times in this book, one of my favorite artist is Bob Marley. I love the strong message of God, spirituality and unity in his music. I think of him as a poet, philosopher, peacemaker and prophet. I think it's amazing how he was able to accomplish so many great things, like uniting political leader Michael Manley and his opponent Edward Seaga, at the 1978 One Love Peace Concert in Kingston, Jamaica…. all through his music.

I listen to his music all the time. One of my favorite songs by Bob is "Three Little Birds". It's an uplifting song about three little birds singing by his doorstep, bringing a message of peace …telling him not to worry because everything is going to be alright.

I will often listen to it if I am going through something or have a problem that I have prayed about. It's a good way to take your mind off whatever is going on, get encouragement and jam at the same time.

I remember one particular time where God used this song to communicate a message of peace to me.

I was sitting on the front porch visiting my dad at his house. It was a bright, sunny day. The sky was clear and there was a cool breeze outside. There were birds flying overhead and we were relaxing and enjoying ourselves. Well... I was trying to enjoy myself.

There was a situation that was worrying me at the time. I can't even remember what it was now, but it was really beginning to steal my joy. I decided that I was not going to let whatever it was chip away at my peace and take away from an otherwise enjoyable day.

Whenever something gets to that point, I know to put on my "God Glasses", like I mentioned earlier, and start looking for anything God may send my way to reassure me. Remember, Jeremiah 29:13 tells us to take action and *"seek"* God and we will find Him.

Well, wouldn't you know, as soon as I decided to take my focus off the problem and "Watch, Hope and Expect" God to show up with a message ... He did!

There is a fence in my dad's yard and I watched as one little bird landed on the fence and stayed there. I didn't really pay it any mind and certainly didn't think of the Bob Marley song; after all it's called "Three Little Birds", not "One Little Bird".

Well, a few minutes later, another little bird landed on the fence right beside the first one. This caught my attention. I thought, *"Okay God, the sky is clear and there are birds flying all over and these two little ones have landed on this fence and have stayed there. If one more little bird lands beside these two, then I'm going to take it as a sign from you. I'm going to chill out and do just what the lyrics of the song say and not worry about a thing ...because you're telling me everything is going to be all right."*

I was watching with anticipation to see what would happen. Would one of the birds fly away before a third could land? Would they both leave? Would a whole group come and land on the fence?

And wouldn't you know, just like clockwork, a third little bird landed on the fence right beside the first two!

Now, it was a nice, sunny day, the sky was clear and there were birds flying all around. Out of all the birds in the sky, these three little ones decided to land right beside each other on the fence facing me and stay there where I could see them.

It was just those three alone, singing away…just like it says in the song. They stayed there for quite awhile with no other birds joining them and none of the three flying away. It was like God was saying, *"Okay, you asked for a sign…bam, there it is …three little birds telling you not to worry, just like in the song."*

This immediately brought a smile to my face because I know God had heard my prayers and was using those three little birds to say, *"Don't worry about a thing, because everything is going be all right!"* And the funniest part about the whole thing is, I can't stand birds! …You can't tell me God doesn't have a sense of humor!

But, that story shows that God can use anything, even something you would never expect, to speak to and reassure you…if you're looking.

This may seem silly, but it's the sort of thing we *have* to start looking for and seeking out. We have no problem accepting every weird little thing that pops into our mind to worry us. Well, how about doing the opposite and looking for something that will help us out? It's often in those things that we will find God.

Like I said earlier, God is not going to come down and physically tap you on the shoulder and say *"Hey, don't worry, this is what you should do."* But, He will use anything He can to get our attention and communicate with us. He knew three little birds sitting alone on a fence singing is something that would grab my attention and remind me of the uplifting lyrics of one of my favorite songs.

Now, that may be something that many of you reading this might not have ever paid any attention to and that's okay! God has a special and unique relationship with each one of His children…. so He may speak to you in an entirely different way.

Some of you have more than one child and I'm sure different things work better when you're trying to get through to each one. It's the same way when God wants to get through to us! I have always loved music, so this is how He will often try and communicate with me. The important thing is that you develop your relationship with God and learn to identify the ways in which He may be trying to speak to *you*.

RIGHTEOUSNESS, THE REMIX- TURN UP THE VOLUME ON GOD !

I'm sure if you go back and look at some of the things that have gone on in your life, you can see where God has tried to speak to you through different things, no matter how big or small. Learning to recognize these things is a huge step in learning to communicate with Him.

I would like everyone reading this to stop and take a moment and think of ways God might be trying to communicate with you. What are some of the different things He could be trying to use to get your attention and speak to you? Once you've come up with a few things, put on your "God Glasses" and start paying attention to those areas in your life.

He could use something you're interested in to speak to you, like movies, music, reading or art. You could be a "people person", so He might try and reach you through others. I even have a friend who has to drive about an hour each way to and from work. During that drive, he looks for anything God may be trying to say to him. Whether, it's something on the radio, a random teaching lesson from a ministry he's loaded on his iPod or a bumper sticker on the car driving in front of him, he uses that time to actively *seek* God out.

This is how we learn to hear from God, get in tune with His "voice" and recognize all the ways He tries to communicate with us.

Many people dismiss things in life as coincidence, luck and chance happenings or don't even acknowledge them at all because they are too busy to take the time to pay attention to the small things.

Can you imagine how many things we miss…just because we aren't looking?

After reading this chapter, I hope you will slow down and take the time to start paying attention to the things that are going on around you, because you never know when or how God may be trying to reach you.

Learning to look at life this way helped me build my faith, strengthen my spirituality, and understand that God is *real* and He really does hear us when we talk to Him. And, He speaks back all the time, we just have to learn to slow down and pay attention. Once we begin to "Watch, Hope and Expect" for Him to show up…He does! I guarantee it.

So, take the first step today and put on your "God Glasses". Once you start looking through them …you just may be surprised at what you see!

SECTION 3

THE POWER OF POSITIVITY

CHAPTER 7

DISCOVER THE POSITIVE!

"It is not what goes into the mouth that defiles a person, but what comes out of the mouth; this defiles a person" (Matthew 15:11, ESV).

In this section, we'll begin talking about something that is a very important factor in our spirituality and relationship with God. It can help us learn how to recognize God when He shows up in our everyday lives (like we talked about in the last chapter). It is crucial for building our faith, learning how to change the way we think, overcoming wrong mindsets, living in peace and is one of the main keys to becoming spiritually successful and living a happy life. It is a power we all have the ability to develop, and once we learn to do so, can change our lives for the better. It is the power of positive thinking.

Proverbs 18:21 tells us that the power of life and death are in the tongue. Whether we realize it or not, our words and thoughts have incredible power and influence over our lives. They shape our outlook and the way we see ourselves and can be used to either build us up or tear us down.

It's just like a domino effect. Our words and thoughts have an impact on how much faith, happiness and peace we have, how we see the world, how we treat others, and how we see our circumstances and potential. A negative way of thinking can knock all of those things down and destroy them without us even realizing it.

The importance of positive thinking is emphasized all throughout The Bible. Proverbs 4:23 (HCSB), warns us, *"Guard your heart above all else, for it is the source of life."* The Good News translation of that scripture tells us to be careful how we think, because our life is shaped by our thoughts.

Also, Matthew 15:11 tells us that it's not what goes *into* the mouth that defiles a person, but what comes *out* of the mouth that defiles a person. I would go a step further and say that it is also what comes out of the mouth that *defines* a person as well. Whether we have a positive or negative outlook in life often determines whether we will succeed or fail.

In this chapter, "Discover the Positive", I want to talk about the importance of having a positive mindset versus a negative one. We'll take a look at how positive thinking is crucial to our spirituality and how a negative mindset can sabotage our growth. We'll also take a look at some of the ways we can go about turning around a negative mindset to change the way we think.

People who have an optimistic or positive way of thinking automatically have many advantages over those who think pessimistically or in a negative way. People who think in a positive way are often happier, more confident, peaceful and less stressed than those who think negatively. They are more powerful, hopeful and often have a stronger faith.

It's impossible for someone to truly believe in the goodness of God and all that He promises us, but be full of negativity and doubt at the same time. It just doesn't work like that.

This doesn't mean that someone who thinks in a positive way glides through life without any problems. It means that when confronted with life's troubles, instead of being consumed by them, they have the ability to pull the positive out of a situation and focus solely on it. Granted, this does take a lot of work. But, by doing so, someone who thinks in a positive way can handle some of life's challenges much better than someone who thinks negatively.

I'm sure everyone reading this knows someone who is upbeat, always has a smile on their face or an encouraging word for others. Well, you might be surprised what that person may be going through or has had to face.

Even though they may face some of the same things in life, a person who has a positive outlook doesn't let the clouds that can sometime come our way dampen their spirit. Instead, they automatically look for the "silver lining". Doing this is how one person can go through something and prosper, while another may go though the same thing and crumble.

Learning to "Discover the Positive" takes effort and practice, but it's something we can all learn to do.

Focusing on the positive in a situation helps us see how good God really is. When faced with difficulties, looking for *anything* positive we can pull out of it, no matter how big or small, gives us something better to hope for and focus on.

On the flip side, when going through things in life, someone who has a negative way of thinking may have thoughts that replay over in their mind like:

- *"I'm not good enough."*
- *"I can never do anything right."*
- *"Things will never change."*
- *"I will never get to where I want to be in life."*
- *"Nothing good ever happens to me."*
- *"I will never get my breakthrough"* or
- *"I will never be healed."*

This way of thinking goes against *everything* God tells us and can go on for years or a person's entire lifetime. This type of thinking can weigh a person down and rob them of any hope they may have for the future. By having a negative mindset and focusing only on the problems life can bring ...is there any wonder why some people walk around looking so miserable or having such a bad attitudes?

Even some Christians have a very negative way of thinking. Even though they may be on a spiritual journey, it's probably a rocky ride that they aren't enjoying very much.

One way we can learn to overcome negative thinking and "Discover the Positive", is to get our thoughts in line with what God tells us, which will sound something like this;

- "*I **am** good enough.*" (Philippians 1:6)
- "*God **does** love me, even while I am changing and growing.*" (Romans 8:1)
- "*Things **will** get better.*" (2 Corinthians 4:17-18)
- "*I **will** get to where I want to be in life as long as I continue to move forward and keep God first.*" (Jeremiah 29:11)
- "*My breakthrough **is** on the way.*" (Romans 8:18)
- "*God's timing is perfect and healing is **mine** through the blood of Jesus!*" (Isaiah 58:8)

And, these declarations are just a few of God's promises!

Now ask yourself; which of these mindsets do you think will get someone further in life?

The challenge for someone who has a negative mindset in learning to get their thoughts in line with what God tells us ...is that it takes faith. We all have faith, which means, "*having complete trust and confidence in someone or something*" (Merriam-Webster.com). However, where we choose to place our faith is completely up to us.

We can choose to place our faith in our circumstances and the negative thoughts that pop into our head or we can choose to place our faith in God and what He tells us in His Word.

Hebrews 11:1(KJV) tells us, "*Faith is the substance of things hoped for, the evidence of things not seen.*"

Many times, people who have a negative way of thinking can only see what's in front of them at the moment. They can't see anything beyond that. So, this is where they place their faith. Their "complete trust and confidence" goes into what they can see only with their eyes... not with their spirit. Again, you wont get very far like that!

I want everyone to stop for a moment and ask yourself:

- "*Where am I placing my faith?*"
- *Where do I put my complete trust and confidence?*"

If the answer is anything other than "in what God has promised me" you may want to be careful. You could be setting yourself up to fail.

In Jeremiah 29:11, the Lord tells us, *"For I know the plans I have for you, plans to prosper you and not to harm you, plans to give you hope and a future."*

Getting our thoughts aligned with that *one* scripture alone can do wonders to help us overcome a negative mindset, look past our circumstances and change the way we think.

Making the *choice* and putting in the *effort* to live this way is important for all aspects of our spirituality.

For example, in the last chapter, "Watch, Hope and Expect", I talked about how God is around us all the time. I talked about how people can miss the ways God tries to communicate with them because they are so busy trying to keep up with the hectic pace of every day life. I talked about how people are moving so fast that they often speed right by God and miss Him when He shows up in their lives.

Well, the same thing can happen if our minds are busy and distracted with negative thoughts. As human beings, we will always have very active minds, but it's up to us which direction they move in. Someone who thinks in a negative way has a mind that is so weighed down with worry, anxiety, judgment, frustration, doubt, guilt, fear and grumbling, that it can cause them to miss anything God tries to use to get their attention, give them comfort and help them.

While writing this section, I watched a documentary on nuns living in a convent and their way of life. They explained why they decide to give up their worldly possessions and devote their lives to Christ. They also explained why they choose to take some of the vows they do. One nun said something very cool when explaining why they spend so much time devoted to praying in silence, which can be as much as seven hours a day.

She said, "The Lord speaks in silence, and in silence is He heard. We must be alert." I felt that was important to include here. It is important for our minds to be as peaceful as possible so we will be able to hear God when He speaks to us.

But someone who thinks in a negative way has a mind that is so distracted and cluttered with "what if's", expecting the worst and replaying the least hopeful scenarios that it clouds their ability to do so.

1 Peter 1:13 (ISV) states, *"Therefore, prepare your minds for action, keep a clear head, and set your hope completely on the grace to be given you when Jesus, the Messiah, is revealed."*

Making the decision to align our thoughts with God's Word helps our minds become more clear and at peace. This way we can get better at hearing His voice and strengthening our spirituality.

Another way we can fight negative thinking is to work on changing our expectations.

If we align our expectations with what God says in His word, we can't help but to expect positive things to happen! As I mentioned in the last chapter, we are supposed to live every day with expectancy and hope. Micah 7:7 tells us that we should wait *expectantly* and confidently for God to show up. There are many scriptures in the Bible like the one from Micah that tell us we are supposed to wake up every morning and *expect* God to show up in our lives with good things.

Psalms 31:24 (AMP) says, *"Be strong and let your heart take courage, all you who wait for, hope for and expect the Lord!"* Psalms 27:14 (AMP) tells us, *"Wait, hope for and expect the Lord; be brave and of good courage and let your heart be stout and enduring. Yes, wait for and hope for and expect the Lord."*

And, Lamentations 3:22 tells us that God's blessings and mercies are new every morning.

A good way to help turn negative thinking around is to wake up every morning and expect God to show up in your life with those blessing and mercies. Living this way is one of the things that makes life as a Christian very exciting!

But, someone who has a negative mindset probably wakes up and expects very different things from their day than someone who thinks in a positive way. A pessimist, by definition, is *"someone who looks towards the least hopeful view of a situation, a person who sees or habitually anticipates the worst"* (Merriam-Webster.com).

How many times have you gotten up on the "wrong side of the bed" and before you even put your feet on the floor thought, *"Great... It's going to be one of those days."* Chances are, it probably was one of "those" days.

This is because starting the day off with negative *thoughts*, gives us negative *expectations*, which gives us negative *experiences*.

Remember, negative thinking is like a domino effect!

We all have days like this from time to time, but some people live their entire lives like this. Something as simple as meditating on the above scriptures from Psalms or saying, "I'm expecting something good to happen to me today", can begin to change and renew a person's entire way of thinking.

If you expect good things to happen throughout your day, then you will begin to notice them when they do. Pretty soon, you will start to see that no matter what negativity you may be faced with, there will always be something positive to focus on too, no matter how big or small. Focusing on these things and holding onto them is what gives us hope.

So, take a minute and ask yourself,

"What am I expecting?"

- Are you expecting God to show up in your life with good things? Or, do you put more faith in your circumstances than you do the goodness of the Lord?
- Is your mind free from worry, doubt, fear, anxiety and frustration so that you are able to recognize Him when He shows up? Or does your way of thinking keep you distracted and weighed down?
- Are your thoughts aligned with God's Word to build you up or are they focused only on what you can see to tear you down?

If you have a mind that is trained to automatically focus in on, magnify and expect the negative, then that is all you will ever see. And, God is many things, but negative is not one of them!

We are all able to turn our thinking around and have a more positive outlook in life. Focusing on the positive takes effort but so does living in the bondage of negative thinking. So, please don't continue to focus on the negative, because if you do, you will never… "Discover the Positive"!

CHAPTER 8

WATCH YOUR WORDS!

"He who guards his mouth and his tongue, guards his soul from troubles"(Proverbs 21:23, NASB).

In the last chapter, we learned how important it is to have a positive outlook on life and how positive thinking plays a huge role in our spirituality. We talked about a few of the ways we can go about turning a negative mindset into a positive one and how doing so will benefit us.

However, once we start doing the work to think in a more positive way, we have to be very careful. The world we live in is not a perfect place. There is negativity all around us. Some of it's right in front of our face, (like what we see on the evening news), while some of it is not so obvious. If we're not careful, there are many *little* ways negativity can creep into our lives and have a big impact on our progress. Being able to recognize it and stop it in its tracks is the key to maintaining the peace of mind and positive outlook we are working so hard to achieve.

In this chapter, "Watch Your Words", I want to talk about one of the major ways we allow negativity to sneak into our lives. You guessed it… through our words. We'll take a look at some prime examples we all face everyday and how they may be having more effect on us than we think. We'll also take a look at what the Bible tells us to do when faced with certain situations involving our words and practical ways we can follow through.

They can be big, little, deliberate or unintentional. They can be meant as a joke, said in passing or part of our everyday conversation.

No matter the context, our words *all* have an impact. However, *what* impact they have is something only we can control.

Proverbs 18:21(ISV) warns us, *"The power of the tongue is life and death— those who love to talk will eat what it produces."*

The International Standard version of that scripture puts it in a very clear way. It lets us know that the words we speak into the atmosphere *will* produce something. However, whether they produce life or death is strictly up to us.

No matter if you are just beginning your spiritual journey or have been on your path for years, you have to pay very careful attention to your words. They can either feed a negative mindset or help you overcome one. Some of the most important scriptures in The Bible are designed to help us find power and positivity through our words.

- ❖ Proverbs 21:23 (NASB) advises, *"He who guards his mouth and his tongue, guards his soul from troubles."*
- ❖ Proverbs 12:14 (NASB) says, *"A man will be satisfied with good by the fruit of his words."*
- ❖ Proverbs 16:24 (ESV) says, *"Gracious words are like a honeycomb, sweetness to the soul and health to the body."*
- ❖ Proverbs 12:18 (NIV) tells us, *"The words of the reckless pierce like swords, but the tongue of the wise brings healing."*

However, many people don't take the time to think about the words they are saying before they say them. They don't realize the impact negative words can have on our way of thinking, even in the simplest situations.

For example, here's a situation I know we have *all* been in. How many of you reading this have ever been in a group of people like co - workers, friends or family members who have been grumbling, complaining or gossiping about something or another? It can be something simple like a new procedure at work, a family dinner that didn't go as planned or that friend who always shows up late and holds everyone else up. It's almost an automatic response to join in and add your two- cents, right?

To some of you, something this small may seem harmless and not very important to your spirituality. It may not seem like a big deal when trying to overcome a negative way of thinking and focus on more positive things. But, this is the sort of thing that can open the door and welcome negativity right back into our lives.

Solomon 2:15 tells us that it is the *little* foxes that spoil the vines. Meaning, the smallest things can add up and do major damage.

Think of it like a huge snowball rolling downhill... all it takes is a few rumbles to get the ball rolling! Negative words have more of an impact on our lives than we think. A simple conversation can affect your mood, attitude and train of thought for the rest of the day. However, The Bible tells us how to avoid this over and over again.

The following scriptures come especially in handy when faced with situations like the ones I described above.

- Philippians 2:14 (NLT) advises us, *"Do everything without complaining and arguing."*
- Colossians 4:6 (ESV) says, *"Let your speech always be gracious, seasoned with salt, so that you may know how you ought to answer each person."*
- Ephesians 4:29 (ESV) says, *"Let no corrupting talk come out of your mouths, but only what is good for building up, as fits the occasion, that it may give grace to those who hear."*
- Job 27:4 (KJV) says, *"My lips will not speak wickedness, Nor my tongue utter deceit."*
- Psalm 39:1(NKJV) says, *"I will guard my ways, Lest I sin with my tongue; I will restrain my mouth with a muzzle, While the wicked are before me."*

It takes a strong person who is serious about their spirituality to set themselves apart from the crowd and not feed into the negativity that may be going on around them. As a matter of fact, you may want to bookmark this page or highlight these scriptures and refer to them often. I know I will!

We're faced with many situations like the examples I gave daily. If you are someone who is struggling with a negative way of thinking, the last thing you should do is surround yourself with negative talk, whether it's coming from yourself or others, no matter how harmless it may seem.

Think about it this way: If you were trying to get in shape and live a healthy lifestyle, you wouldn't sit around all day and eat a bunch of junk food. You would try to stay away from cookies, cake, chips and soda. Those are "empty" calories, meaning they do you no good. Putting that sort of thing in your body would hurt your progress and may undo what you are trying to achieve, correct?

Well, if we are trying to get our thoughts in shape and develop a healthier way of thinking, then why would we sit around and listen to or take part in a bunch of grumbling, complaining, gossip and fault-finding? Those are "empty" words that do us absolutely no good!

The same way "empty" calories can have a negative impact on our health and the way we feel, "empty" words can have a negative impact on our attitude, mood and the way we think. Just like a person who lives a healthy lifestyle watches what they eat and makes sure every calorie counts, a person who has a healthy mindset watches what they say and makes sure every word counts!

I want everyone reading this to try something. The next time you are in a situation like the one I described…I challenge you to do something about it. No, you don't have to run screaming from the room like an idiot with your hands over your ears. Just practice this one simple saying that we have all heard a million times, *"If you don't have anything nice to say…then don't say anything at all!"*

It might be difficult at first, but remember, Romans 12:2 (ESV) tells us, *"Do not be conformed to this world, but be transformed by the renewal of your mind."* The New Living Translation of that verse begins, *"Don't copy the behavior and customs of this world, but let God transform you into a new person by changing the way you think."*

I guarantee you, your silence will speak volumes and other people will start to see that you are someone who doesn't tolerate negativity. Pretty soon, they will not come to you with grumbling, complaining, gossip and confusion because their negativity won't have anything to feed off!

This reminds me of a friend of mine that I have known for years. She is a very nice girl who, I believe, deep down has a good heart. She is the type of girl who goes to church every Sunday and even volunteers to help clean up the church on weekends.

We started off as close friends but have grown apart over the years. This is because every time we would talk, she had a constant habit of gossiping and talking trash about other people. Now, even before I started working on my spirituality, that was never my thing. I have always been too focused on the things I was trying to do to worry about other people and what they were doing.

When she would call, I would just listen. I would never ask any questions, co-sign her opinions or give her *anything* negative to feed off.

My words were always positive and encouraging as I shared with her some of the same type of things I am sharing with you all in this chapter. Of course, that wasn't what she wanted to hear. So, she started calling less and less… which was a win for me!

Now, on the rare occasion when we talk, our conversations have gotten better and are on a much higher level. I actually enjoy talking to her once in a while. But, in order to get to that point, I had to let it be known I am not the type of person you can come to with that sort of negativity.

I want everyone reading this to stop right now and ask yourself, *"What do the words I speak and the words I am willing to listen to say about me?"*

If you don't like the answer, then take a stand, make your words count and stop letting your mind become a trash dump for everything people bring your way. It has a greater effect on you than you think!

One sad thing my experiences with that friend showed me is that many Christians go to church every Sunday and say they believe in God, but never experience any significant breakthroughs in happiness, peace or joy, simply because they are negative.

I won't go into it too deeply in this chapter but I believe one of the main reasons some people don't want anything to do with God or what it means to be a believer is because they have come into contact with a negative, doubtful, complaining, gossiping, judgmental Christian.

To someone who knows very little about the Lord, this can be a turning point in his or her journey. During some of those conversations with my friend, I kept thinking, *"This is ridiculous. You sit in church every Sunday, can quote Bible verses backwards and forward and say you're a Christian...but this is how you represent God and what it means to be a believer? If this is how some of His representatives act, then no wonder some people go running in the opposite direction!"*

Having a negative mindset and expectations is harmful enough, but letting that negativity come through in our words, attitude and how we treat other people is especially damaging for Christians.

We are supposed to be examples to the world. We are supposed to shed a good light on what it means to be a believer. We are supposed to be different. But, we cannot do this if we fall victim to a negative way of thinking. Having a negative mindset that is expressed through grumbling, complaining, gossiping, judging and finding fault does nothing to shed light on Gods name or to make anyone else want to take part in what we believe in.

James 1:26 (NLT) says, *"If you claim to be religious but don't control your tongue, you are fooling yourself, and your religion is worthless."*

If you are reading this and you consider yourself to be a Christian, I want you to stop and ask yourself:

- "What type of words am I speaking and why?"
- "Are they negative or positive?"
- "Do they build me up or tear me down?"
- "Are they helpful to others?"
- "Do they make people want to be around me or get away as fast as they can?"
- "Do they encourage my dreams or tear them down?"
- "Are they full of gossip and lies or are they trustworthy?"
- "Do they set me apart from others or make me just like the rest of the world?"

If you are convicted by some of the answers, then you might need to make some changes.

If we think about it hard enough, we have all seen examples of how powerful words can be. There are countless talk shows where people want to confront the bullies that picked on them years ago. They come on television to show how hard they have worked to prove they aren't all those negative things they were called when they were younger. They come back to show off new bodies to prove they weren't "fat" or "lazy". They come back with successful jobs to show they weren't "dumb" or "stupid". The list goes on and on. In todays world, there are even kids who commit suicide because of the negative things people say about them online. Words are very powerful ...so we have to be also!

Many people might say, "They should just get over it!" Well, depending on your mindset, that's easier said than done. How many of you reading this right now can think of at least one person you know who grew up hearing horrible, negative things? Maybe, it was even you who heard those types of things. Some adults hold onto that negativity their entire lives. This is a perfect example of how damaging negative words can be.

People who grew up hearing negative things about themselves either do one of two things: turn out to be exactly what they told they were growing up or fight hard to overcome that negativity and prove otherwise. Negative words are so powerful that they can become a person's only motivation throughout their entire life!

This reminds me of a television show I watched not too long ago. It was about parents who encouraged their children's dreams of playing basketball, in hopes they would become the next Lebron James or Steph Curry. The kids would practice everyday with coaches and get good advice. What I noticed is that many of the kids would actually play pretty well ... as long as some of their parents weren't around.

There was this one kid in particular, he was dedicated, focused, listened to the coaches and made some really good progress. However, when his dad would pull him to the side and give him a "pep talk" before he went on the court, the kid would be a mess.

His dad would say things like, "You still have a long way to go compared to these other kids. I'm not sure if you'll ever be as good as they are." He even told him, "Every time you get the ball in your hands, I get nervous." I was watching it thinking, *"What kind of pep talk is this??"*

And sure enough, when the kid would get on the court, he would drop the ball, miss shots and play worse than he ever had. Even though, he would play well when the coaches encouraged him and gave him feedback, when his dad showed up with only negative things to say, he would crumble.

I'm sure his dad didn't mean any harm. Maybe he was just talking to his son the only way he knew how? Maybe that's the way his parents had talked to him? By the end of the show, even the coaches had recognized the pattern and called it out.

If you recall, in the last chapter, I said negativity is like a domino effect. Not only can it affect how much faith, happiness and peace we have in our own lives, but it can also affect those around us, sometimes for generations!

The scary part about some of the examples in this chapter is that most people do them every day without even realizing it!

Complaining, grumbling, fault finding, judging other people, gossiping, and listening to this sort of talk throws the door wide open for negativity to creep right back into our lives. Whether we realize it or not, negative words have an impact on us spiritually and will only hinder any progress we are trying to make to turn our thoughts around and think in a more positive way.

If this sounds like something you're having trouble with, please don't continue to be a victim of the hidden negativity that may be in your words. Remember what the Bible says in Proverbs 21:23, *"He who guards his mouth and his tongue, guards his soul from troubles."* Start to practice what it says in Philippians 2:14, and do everything without complaining or arguing, grumbling or disputing. It may take some practice, but the results will amaze you.

Don't continue to speak or listen to "empty" words, instead begin to "Watch Your Words" and take a *stand* for yourself and the positive changes you want to make in your life. It will definitely be worth it!

CHAPTER 9

STOP, LOOK & LISTEN

"Whoever walks with the wise becomes wise, but the companion of fools will suffer harm" (Proverbs 13:20,ESV).

As you can see from the past few chapters, having a positive outlook in life is very important. It is important to our spirituality, peace of mind and even has an effect on those around us. By focusing on God's Word, we can all learn to turn negative thoughts around and develop a more positive way of thinking.

Learning to change our expectations (Lamentations 3:22), align our thoughts with what God says (Jeremiah 29:11) and watch the way we speak (Proverbs 18:21) can do wonders in helping us experience the power of positivity in our lives.

But, what happens once we get all of those things in order? What else can we do to ensure our progress in maintaining a positive attitude? What's the next step? Well, as you know, we don't live in this world alone. We are surrounded by people and have to deal with others on a daily basis.

As you begin to work towards having a more positive outlook in life, you may start to see that not everyone is on the same page as you. If you are not careful, you can allow other people to have a negative impact on your progress and drag you down with their way of thinking. This is another way negativity can creep right back into our lives, even as we're trying to change.

So, unless you plan on moving to a deserted island and not having any more human contact, the next step in maintaining positivity in your life may be to start re-evaluating some of the people around you!

We may not have control of many things in life, but taking a long look at the company we choose to keep and making some necessary changes is one way to help us maintain the positivity we're trying to achieve.

In this chapter, "Stop, Look & Listen", I want to talk about how important it is to *Stop*…take a long *Look* at the people around you …and *Listen* to what's coming out of their mouth. We'll look at some key scriptures that encourage us to choose our company wisely and ways we can go about doing so.

Once you start doing this, you'll learn very quickly that the people around you fall into one of two categories:

- Those who help your progress and
- Those who hinder it

Once you identify who's who, it will be easier to make some changes!

Once we make the decision to pursue our spirituality and think in a more positive way, we automatically become more aware of the negativity coming from others around us, even if we never noticed it before.

2 Corinthians 5:17 (GW) tells us, "*Whoever is a believer in Christ is a new creation. The old way of living has disappeared. A new way of living has come into existence.*"

1 Peter 1:3 (NLT) says, "*All praise to God, the Father of our Lord Jesus Christ. It is by his great mercy that we have been born again.*"

Many of you reading this are parents. When your child was first born, I'm sure you were very particular about who they were around, where you took them and what they were exposed to.

Well, if the Bible tells us that we are new creations and have also been born again… why should we be any different with who we're around and what we're exposed to?

If we have the wrong type of people around us, they can kill our dreams, damage our self esteem, take away our motivation and fill us with negativity...all by just opening their mouth!

For example, I have a good friend who recently got accepted into one of the best schools for Music Engineering and Production, Full Sail. He has been trying to get into this school for a while and finally got the resources to go. When he found out he was accepted, he was excited and wanted to tell everyone about it. When he told me, I congratulated him because I know how badly he wanted to go. He thanked me and then told me when he mentioned it to another person he knew, that person responded, "I don't know why you want to go there, I know a lot of people who went there and it didn't help them at all."

Whether that's true or not is not the point. That person's negative comment had an impact on my friend and took away some of his excitement because he felt the need to tell me about it.

Those few words could have easily turned into something to make him doubt his whole decision to even go to school. And, in a lot of people it does. Some people never grow spiritually, pursue their dreams, live in peace, have a happy life or reach their true potential just because they have negative people around them.

I have known this friend for years and he always encourages other people in their dreams and goals. I have told him time and time again that he won't always get the same thing in return. You have to be very careful who you choose to share these sorts of things with. Everyone is not going to be happy for you and a negative person can become a "dream killer" with just a few words!

Proverbs 21:5 (ESV) tells us, *"The plans of the diligent lead to abundance, but everyone who is hasty comes only to poverty."*

Whoever this was that my friend decided to share his good news with was hasty to speak, not taking the time to think about the negative effect their words would have on him. This person had evidently never heard the phrase, "It's not what you say, but how you say it."

Thankfully, my friend had the good sense not to be discouraged by this person and to continue on with his plan. Now, he is following his dreams, doing well in school and enjoying his classes.

This is just a small example of the sort of thing we have to be aware of when dealing with other people. If you can think of someone in your life who always reacts negatively when you share good things with them, then it may be time to stop, take a closer look at that person and ask yourself, *"Why are they even around in the first place?"*

I remember years ago, when I first started going to the studio and recording music, I would play new songs for my friends and talk about my dreams of one day making it in the music industry. Many times, I would be met by blank stares and would receive very little feedback or encouragement. I would receive more support from the people in the industry I was working with and even from strangers than I would from the people I was close to at the time. They would be the ones to tell me to keep going and that I had what it takes to make it.

Despite never being able to figure out why the people I considered my "friends" would never support me, I kept moving forward and being diligent, like it says to in Proverbs 21:5.

It wasn't until the day I shot my first music video, "Get Dat Doe", (which I'm sure is still on YouTube somewhere, lol), that I learned why they acted the way they did. Tons of people showed up for the shoot and everyone that I did music with was there to support me. But, none of my close friends bothered to show up.

After the shoot, I was talking to the director and he asked me if I was happy with the way everything turned out. When I told him about my friends, how they hadn't bothered to show up and the reactions (or lack of) I would get from them when I talked about my music and my dreams, he told me something that I still remember to this day. He said, "You can't speak success to people who aren't about it."

Needless to say, that was a huge lesson for me. Immediately, I made some changes. Ever since then, I have been very careful who I have chosen to share my dreams and goals with. Even when writing this book, only the people closest to me knew I was writing it and have encouraged and supported me along the way.

It may seem like a drastic approach when dealing with people but when we are trying to build something in life, we cannot afford to be surrounded with people who don't support us and will tear it down with negativity.

I'm sure we all know people like this. We run across them all the time in everyday life. They could be our bosses, co- workers and even family members. The difference is, most of the time, we can't choose any of those people. Your boss is your boss, you work with whoever is in your department and your family will always be your family. But, choosing to call these types of people "friends" and surround ourselves with them does us more harm than good when we are trying to make changes for the better and focus on the positive things in life.

I want you to take a minute and ask yourself:

- *"Do I know anyone like this?"*
- *"Am I around anyone who doesn't support me and kills my dreams?"*
- *"Am I spending my time with anyone who is negative, bitter, angry or jealous?"*

If the answer to any of those questions is "yes", the more important question is.... *"Why?"*

Proverbs 27:17 (NIV) tells us, *"As iron sharpens iron, so one person sharpens another."*

It is important to keep people around us who are positive, encouraging, supportive, goal oriented and focused. We have to spend our time with those who help us maintain positivity, peace of mind and work towards what we are trying to accomplish, not those who work against it.

While some people have been placed in our path so we might be able to help them along even as we are growing and learning, this is not always the case. Some people simply don't want to be happy or have not yet made the decision to do so. Some people thrive off negativity and can spread it to others. It is very important we learn to tell the difference!

This brings up a great example. I have a buddy of mine that I have known for years. Deep down, he's good guy and always willing to help when needed. However, I don't hang out with him a lot or spend too much time with him because he is the sort of person who feeds off negativity.

I learned this early on and am reminded of it every time I log onto Facebook. When his post show up in my news feed, they're filled with pictures of people he sees when he's out and about, snaps a picture of, posts online and makes negative comments about. He even goes as far as to type out conversations he has with co- workers, friends or even random people. He gives a play by play of what they say to him and how he comes back with an insult or something smart to tear them down.

Now, we all have incidents like this with other people from time to time, but choosing to go out of your way and post them online is not a very good way to represent yourself. He isn't a bad person at all, but you would never know it from some of the negativity he projects. Even my mom noticed his posts online and said something to me about it!

This is the type of thing, if we're not careful, we can be drawn into. When he makes a post online, it's obvious by the comments and "likes", that other people are drawn into his negativity, which only encourages him to post more of the same. Can you imagine being surrounded by these types of people everyday in real life?

I remember an incident years ago when I was hanging out with him. We were waiting in line at a store and the line was extremely long. There was one employee behind the counter, who was struggling to keep up with all the customers. Everyone was sympathetic to the employee and waiting patiently...except my friend. He was grumbling, complaining, making smart comments and being downright negative. He kept going on until I couldn't take it any more and said, "Look, we're all waiting in the same line, there is *one* person behind the counter. Everyone is being patient but you, now either shut up or get out of the line!"

Now, I admit, what I said probably wasn't right either, but his negativity had begun to take a toll on me. Remember, I mentioned earlier, the more you make the decision to think in a positive way, the more you will become aware of the negativity coming from others? Well, that's a perfect example.

I was trying to think in a positive way despite the long wait and his negativity was working against that. His complaining began to sound like nails on a chalkboard and I couldn't take it any more.

Again, it's not that he's a bad guy. He would do anything in the world for his friends and vice versa. It's just that he projects negativity. And, for the sake of our peace of mind, we have to limit the amount of time we spend with people like that.

In John 14:27(NLT), Jesus says, *"I am leaving you with a gift...peace of mind and heart. And the peace I give is a gift the world cannot give. So don't be troubled or afraid."*

Our peace of mind is a very valuable gift and is crucial for staying positive and strengthening our spirituality. However, some people never experience this gift simply because they let others chip away at it.

Some people spend their entire lives in bad relationships, friendships and discouraged by the negative people around them and wonder why they are not happy or have not had any sort of breakthrough in their life. People do this for all sorts of reasons:

- Some people are afraid to be alone and figure having a negative person around them is better than having no one at all.
- Some people are equally as negative and don't realize having these type of people around is even a problem. (Remember the saying "misery loves company"?)
- Others gain their self worth by having lots of "friends", even the ones who may be doing them more harm than good.

I'm sure I could write another whole book on how people find themselves in all sorts of bad situations because of the company they keep. But, the Bible gives us great advice on many things, including how to avoid falling into these types of situations.

- ❖ Proverbs 22:24-25 (NIV) tells us, *"Do not make friends with a hot-tempered man, do not associate with one easily angered, or you may learn his ways and get yourself ensnared."*

- ❖ Titus 3:10 (ESV) tells us, *"As for a person who stirs up division, after warning him once and then twice, have nothing more to do with him."*
- ❖ Proverbs 18:24 (ESV) says, *"A man of many companions may come to ruin, but there is a friend who sticks closer than a brother."*
- ❖ 1Corinthians 15:33 (ESV) says, *"Do not be deceived: bad company ruins good morals."*

And, when it comes to choosing friends, my father likes to say; "I'd rather have one or two dependable cars in my driveway than a yard full of junk cars that aren't going anywhere." Meaning, when it comes to people, *quantity* does not always equal *quality*!

Over the years, I have learned to keep all these things in mind when choosing the company I keep. In doing so, I have learned the importance of having positive minded people in my circle. I like to think of it this way: there are two types of people in the world, those who add to your peace of mind and those who take away from it.

Knowing the difference and having the courage to do something about it could mean the difference between your success and failure!

My mother likes to say that I refuse to let anyone rent any "space" in my head. This is very true!

It's like the Bob Marley song, "Satisfy My Soul", where he sings about sailing along smoothly and asks that you please don't rock his boat. I look at life and friendship this way. If you reach a point in your life where you are "sailing" along smoothly and someone comes into your life, and your boat starts to rock … that person has to go!

If some people just went through the contact list in their phone and deleted some names, they may see a huge difference in their lives! It certainly has helped me in achieving all the things I set out to do. And, I know it can help you as well!

So, start by asking yourself:

- "What type of company do I keep?"
- "Is there anyone around me who causes confusion, is negative and takes away from my peace of mind?"

- *"Who encourages my hopes and dreams and who tears them down?"*
- *"Am I a better person because of the people around me or am I worse off?"*

Some of the answers may surprise you!

Remember, Proverbs 13:20 says, *"Whoever walks with the wise becomes wise, but the companion of fools will suffer harm."* So, take a moment to "Stop, Look & Listen" to the people around you. You'll be able to tell very quickly if you're walking with the wise or if you are a companion of fools.

Depending on the answer ... it may be time to make some changes!

SECTION 4
SPIRITUAL WARFARE

CHAPTER 10

THE BATTLE WITHIN

"We do not wrestle against flesh and blood, but against the rulers, against the authorities, against the cosmic powers over this present darkness, against the spiritual forces of evil in the heavenly places" (Ephesians 6:12, ESV).

Over the past few chapters, we have been talking about the power of positivity. We've seen how important it is to have a positive mindset, to watch the way we speak, to recognize negativity coming from ourselves and others and to surround ourselves with people who help our progress and not hinder it. All of these things are extremely important because they play a huge part in helping us win a much *bigger* battle.

It is a battle we all go through everyday to some degree, no matter who we are, where we live, how much money we have or how "spiritual" we consider ourselves to be. It is a battle we are all engaged in whether we realize it or not and if we have a negative way of thinking, can tear us down that much quicker.

It is not the sort of battle that's fought in a far off country with tanks and machine guns, but it's just as deadly. It is the battle in our mind …the battle against our very own thoughts.

Now, you may be thinking, *"Well, if I work on changing my mindset and getting rid of negativity around me…. then I shouldn't have too much of a problem with negative thoughts"*, right?

While all of the things we have been talking about so far certainly help us fight this battle, we are up against an enemy who will never leave us alone and will always target our thoughts to try and drag us down and destroy us.

1 Peter 5:8 (ESV), tells us, *"Be sober-minded; be watchful. Your adversary the devil prowls around like a roaring lion, seeking someone to devour."* Ephesians 6:12 explains, *"We do not wrestle against flesh and blood, but against the rulers, against the authorities, against the cosmic powers over this present darkness, against the spiritual forces of evil in the heavenly places."* And John 8:44, says, *"the devil is a liar and the father of all lies."*

While it is God's intent for us to have great lives, accomplish our dreams, live in peace, abundance and be powerful individuals, it is the enemy's plan to see just the opposite. It is his goal to hold us back, keep us in bondage and to do all he can to stop us from becoming the people God created us to be.

He can try to accomplish this plan in many ways. Almost anything can be used to try and steal our joy, kill our dreams or destroy our faith. He can work through circumstances in our life, bad habits or behaviors that may be holding us back and even other people.

While all of these things have the potential to help him do his job, no attack is more damaging than the one he wages against our thoughts.

If the enemy gets ahold of our mind, he can attack our peace, our self worth, our hope, our faith...the list goes on and on. If we allow him to set up shop in our mind, the effects can be just as devastating as any war that's fought in the physical world!

In this chapter, "The Battle Within", I want to talk more about the enemy's plan against us and how he tries to carry it out by attacking our thoughts. We'll take a look at some of the tactics he uses and how they can have devastating effects on our life. 2 Corinthians 11:3 (ESV), tells us, *"I am afraid that as the serpent deceived Eve by his cunning, your thoughts will be led astray from a sincere and pure devotion to Christ."* The devil has declared war on us and his biggest target is our mind. However, the most dangerous part of his plan is that most people aren't even aware of it!

For instance, while doing research for this chapter, I found that the average human being has around 50,000 thoughts per day. Some experts estimate that almost 70-80% of those thoughts are negative.

This gives the enemy a huge opportunity to use our thoughts as his playground to plant all sorts of seeds of deception, insecurity, negativity and lies. Now, do you understand why we spent so much time in the last section talking about positivity?

Many people don't know we are able to fight back against the enemy's attacks on our mind. They have fallen into the trap of believing horrible things about themselves and their lives. Many people just accept the devil's lies as the truth and live their lives accordingly.

Millions of people live their lives in bondage, addiction, have low self esteem, no self worth, are in bad relationships and put limits on their potential and what they can achieve just because they believe the lies the enemy feeds them. This is what I mean when I say some people aren't even aware there is a battle going on and more importantly … that they're losing!

Many people don't understand that we have a choice in how we think and what thoughts we choose to accept. They don't realize that not every thought that comes into our mind is the truth. Many of them are lies sent by the devil. Those thoughts are like *"flaming arrows fired by the evil one"*, (Ephesians 6:16, NASB) and just like real arrows …they are meant to destroy!

2 Corinthians 10:5 (ESV), tells us we should *"destroy arguments and every lofty opinion raised against the knowledge of God and take every thought captive to obey Christ."* In other words, we need to start taking a closer look at our thoughts to identify which ones are helping us and which ones are hurting us.

I remember when I first realized this. Since, I don't go to church and have decided to pursue my spirituality in other ways, I do a lot of reading. My favorite preacher, Joyce Meyer, wrote a very powerful book called *The Battlefield of the Mind*. In it, the first thing she did was quote John 8:44, *"The devil is a liar."* It's a simple sentence. However, taking the time to *really* understand that one scripture changed my whole life. Until then, I never considered that some of the thoughts running through my mind were simply *not true*.

That was the first time I understood all the negative thoughts I had about myself, my future and never being able to achieve my dreams and goals were not true. That was the first time I realized that my negative attitude and frustration came from *believing* those lies. It was the first time I was able to recognize all the good things going on around me, how much I was blessed and how much potential I had. It was like a blindfold was lifted and I was finally able to see the truth!

This was also the first time I realized that there was a serious battle going on and the enemy's only purpose was to destroy me with his lies.

Once we understand that the devil uses our thoughts against us, we can begin to separate what's true from the nonsense that pops into our head sometimes. Being able to do this will give you a new perspective and can change your entire life. I know it did for me!

The Bible identifies Satan over and over as a deceiver, a schemer and a liar. Well, if we know that the devil is a liar, his only goal is to destroy us and he does this by attacking our mind...why do so many people still fall for it? How is he able to have such a strong grip on the way some people think?

One way he is able to do this is by building up "strongholds" in people's minds. There are many definitions of the word "stronghold". It can mean *"a place of confinement; a prison"*, *"a binding power and influence"* or *"a fortified place; a fort or castle"* (1913 Webster).

When it comes to our thoughts, I believe Joyce Meyer has a great definition, which is *"areas of thinking not based on truth, but lies, which instead of protect us, imprison us."*

A stronghold is called that because that's exactly what it is ...a *strong hold*. Some people believe the enemy's lies for so long, certain areas of their thinking can turn into "places of confinement" ...and they become prisoners in their own mind.

Any type of thinking that holds us captive, chains us down and hinders us from moving forward boldly and with confidence toward what God has planned for our lives can be considered a stronghold.

These ways of thinking can be used by the enemy to hold us back in many different ways.

Some examples of strongholds and the roadblocks they can lead to in our lives are:

- ❖ *Insecurity* …which can lead to developing wrong relationships, comparing ourselves to others and feelings of inadequacy.
- ❖ *Jealousy* …which can lead to gossip, being judgmental and spitefulness.
- ❖ *Bitterness* …which can lead to unforgiveness, anger and resentment.
- ❖ *Fear* …which can lead to inability to reach our goals and a lack of faith.
- ❖ *Rejection* …which can lead to forming addictions, seeking acceptance and feelings of unworthiness.

These ways of thinking are designed to hold us back from all the good things God has planned for our life. The enemy can use any one of them to attack us, if we allow him to.

We can have strongholds built up in our mind regarding ourselves, others, and even about God. Many people walk around with strongholds in their mind that affect their lives and choices everyday, not realizing that they are an open doorway for the enemy to work.

Can you think of any areas in your mind, which you've allowed the devil to come in and use against you?

I bet everyone reading this can think of at least one area where the enemy has tried to create a stronghold in the way you think in order to hold you back. It may be something like fear, doubt or an attack on your self worth. Some of you may not have realized until *just now* that the devil has set up shop in your mind and is attacking you from within!

Now, you may be wondering… *"How are these strongholds formed?"* or *"How can someone allow their own thoughts turn into such a powerful force that works against them?"*

Since these ways of thinking are meant to have a harmful effect on our lives, the enemy will often take his time to carefully construct them in our minds. These ways of thinking can take years to develop and can be the result of many things. The way we were raised, having negative people around us or something that has happened to us in our life are all things that can be used by the enemy to shape certain beliefs in us.

He can use those beliefs to keep us in fear, make us think we're not good enough, to think that we could never be blessed or that God (or anyone else for that matter) could never love us ...his list of lies is endless! He can use those lies torture us, affect the choices we make and put us on a path in life towards our own destruction!

Many times, the enemy begins to prowl around when a person is young to look for ways to build a stronghold in the way they think. Everything from a person being bullied, to having parents who talk down to or mistreat them, or being physically abused to a variety of other things can be used by the enemy to begin to form some sort of stronghold in the way a person thinks. Without knowing how to fight back, these thoughts can torment someone their entire life.

The enemy knows the earlier we become a prisoner to any sort of stronghold in the way we think, the easier it will be for him to use it to hold us back, distract us or in the worst cases… destroy us. He looks for, what I like to call, "cracks in the foundation", magnifies them, and then sits back and watches us do the rest of the work for him. And without knowing any better, many people go right along with his plan!

This brings up a conversation I had with a buddy of mine that shows how sneaky the enemy can be when looking for something to use early on in a persons life. This particular buddy of mine has two daughters, both, which are middle school age. We were talking about how he had begun giving them both "the talk" about boys. He told them how important it is that they value themselves, have self worth and be smart enough not to fall for just anything someone tells them. I have been friends with this guy for years and he has always been a big part of his children's lives. I have seen him have talks like this with his kids ever since they were little.

We started talking about how important it is for children, especially girls, to hear these sorts of things from a young age.

I pointed out how the enemy can take advantage of the fact that some people never had this type of validation growing up. He can use the fact that some people never heard anyone tell them that they are special, have worth and should be valued, to affect their confidence. This makes it easy for him to create a stronghold, such as insecurity, in the way they think.

He can then use that way of thinking as an open doorway to destroy how they feel about themselves and affect the choices they make in their life. Believing that you are not good enough can send a person looking for validation in all sorts of wrong directions!

It's pretty clear from just looking at some of the videos posted on the Internet that there are tons of people out there searching for validation and attention in all sorts of ways. Think about all the ridiculous "Challenge" videos we've seen pop up in the past few years on social media alone. And, that's the least of it ...people find themselves in all kinds of undesirable situations because the enemy lies to them and has them wasting time searching for something that only God can provide!

I'm sure everyone reading this knows of someone who keeps going back to a bad relationship or keeps choosing the wrong type of person to be with. This is because the enemy has them convinced they don't deserve any better. As long as they remain a prisoner to those thoughts ... the devil will always have them right where he wants them.

And, that's just *one* example of how the enemy can creep around looking for something to use against us. There are countless examples of how people become prisoners to their own thinking and find themselves on all sorts of paths far from the one God has intended for their life.

We fall into these kinds of traps all the time. We let the enemy convince us of all sorts of things. We let him build strongholds in our mind that affect the way we feel about ourselves, the choices we make in life and even about God's love! We let him convince us we don't deserve better in life or could never accomplish anything great.

Even while writing this book, the enemy came against me in many ways. He attacked my mind with doubt, fear and uncertainty. He attacked my mind with thoughts of, *"Should I really be doing this?" "Will anyone listen to what I have to say?" "Look at all the things I missed out on* and had to give up in order to write this book." "Will it even be worth it?" And my favorite... "After all my hard work...this book might end up in the bargain bin at the Dollar Store!"

Any one of those thoughts could have stopped me right in my tracks. The difference now though, is that I recognize those thoughts as attacks from the enemy and I have learned to fight back!

Any time he would shoot one of those "flaming arrows" at me, I would fire right back with, *"This is something God told me to do, so I'm going to do it." "These are lessons God wants to get to people, and He chose me to do it." "Even if one person is helped by something I said, then it's worth it!"* And, *"Even if this book does end up in the bargain bin at the Dollar Store...it will be the best, most powerful one there and will reach more people!"*

We have to begin to fight back against the lies the enemy tells us. We have to learn to press forward or we will never see all the great things God has planned for our life.

We must begin to do what 2 Corinthians 10:5 tells us and *"destroy arguments and every lofty opinion raised against the knowledge of God, and take every thought captive to obey Christ."*

If we don't learn to take these types of thoughts captive, then we will be the ones who remain prisoners! We will always be at the mercy of the devil and his attacks on our mind and we cannot afford that. Our salvation, hope and future depend on how hard we fight!

If you have been plagued by these type of thoughts, don't worry ...there's nothing wrong with you! Everyone goes through this battle in some way or another. Each one of us is up against an enemy who will never give up, so we can't either!

The good news is, as you keep reading this section, you will see that God has already given us everything we need to fight back and win... "The Battle Within!"

CHAPTER 11

POWER AND AUTHORITY

"I have given you the authority to trample on snakes and scorpions and to overcome all the power of the enemy; nothing will harm you"(Luke 10:19, NIV).

When you think of the words "power" and "authority", what comes to mind? You may associate those words with a person having money, fame, a high-ranking position or a prestigious last name like Rockefeller or Kennedy. You may think of more entertaining times when Donald Trump was just the guy sitting behind a table in a boardroom with a sour look on his face barking at people, "You're fired!" or a person having assistants, employees and a successful business empire.

In a sense, you would be right on target. In the world we live in, those are all things that are associated with a person having power and authority. Oftentimes, people with great amounts of power and authority are highly respected, favored and sometimes even feared.

Take Donald Trump for instance. I never thought when I used him as an example in this chapter that he would go from a boardroom on The Apprentice to the White House in DC. Some may say that the power and authority he held before running for office helped him win the Presidency.

In the business world, it might take a person all of their life to try and achieve that type of status. However, as believers in Christ, we have an even more valuable kind of power available to us *right now*. We have the *power* to live in peace, happiness, to be healthy, confident and fearless and the *authority* to trample all over the enemy. We just have to become comfortable using it.

In the last chapter, I talked about the spiritual battle that we all are engaged in on some level or another. I talked about the enemy we are up against and how he will stop at nothing to destroy us.

At the end of that chapter, I told you not to worry, because God has already given us everything we need to fight back and win that battle. Now, it's time to take a look at what I mean.

In this chapter, "Power and Authority", I want to help you become aware of all the power and authority we have been given as God's children. I want to talk about the major differences between the two. I'll share tips to help you get in touch with your power and strengthen it. We'll also look at how we can become comfortable and confident enough to exercise the authority we have been given to put it all in motion.

People who are successful in the business world may have the power to be respected, favored and feared…but so do we! We have the power to be *respected* by others, *favored* by God and *feared* by the enemy. It's time we started putting it to use!

The first thing that happens once we accept Christ as our savior and let Him into our lives is that we are "adopted" into His family. Ephesians 1:5 (NLT) tells us, *"God decided in advance to adopt us into his own family by bringing us to himself through Jesus Christ. This is what he wanted to do, and it gave him great pleasure."*

Just like a child who is legally adopted into a family is entitled to all the rights, benefits and inheritance of that family, the same goes for us once we are "adopted" by God. We share Jesus's name and as Christians, have access to the power of the Holy Spirit and are able to be more than conquerors.

I like to think of it this way; a billionaire like Donald Trump has several children. Even before he became president, his employees would probably snap to attention when any of them walked into the room. When it comes to his businesses, his children have power, command the same respect and have the same authority to get things done as their father. Well, if they hold that much power because of who *their* father is ... imagine how much power we command because of who *our* Heavenly Father is! Also, keep in mind I'm just using him as an example. It by no means indicates that I support the work (or lack thereof) he's doing in the White House.

The Bible tells us time and again of the power we have through the Holy Spirit. Psalms 68:35 (NLT) tells us, *"God is awesome in his sanctuary. The God of Israel gives power and strength to his people. Praise be to God!"*

Isaiah 40:29-31 (NLT) assures us, *"He gives power to the weak and strength to the powerless. Even youths will become weak and tired, and young men will fall in exhaustion. But those who trust in the Lord will find new strength. They will soar high on wings like eagles. They will run and not grow weary. They will walk and not faint."*

1 Corinthians 15:57 (NLT) tells us, *"But thank God! He gives us victory over sin and death through our Lord Jesus Christ."* And, 2 Timothy 1:7 (NIV) tells us, *"For the Spirit God gave us does not make us timid, but gives us power, love and self-discipline."*

As joint heirs with Christ (Romans 8:17), we have the power to overcome many things including Satan and all his schemes! However, many people, including Christians, still fall victim to his traps. Why is that? Well, there are a few things we need to understand in order to be able to put up a good fight.

I want to start by looking at the words "power" and "authority". They are very different. I could quote Bible scriptures all day about how God will crush Satan under our feet (Romans 16:20), how we can resist the devil and he will flee (James 4:7) or how we can put on the full armor of God and take a stand against the devil (Ephesians 6:11). However, hearing about all that power will do us absolutely no good, if we don't exercise the *authority* we have to put it to use!

Think about it like this: Having power without exercising the *authority* to put it to use is like having a police officer who sits in his car all day. There might be robberies going on around him, people running red lights, cars being stolen and a million other crimes taking place. He has been given the power to stop it all but how much good does it do ...if he never gets out of the car and exercises his authority to enforce it? The same thing applies to us in our battle against Satan.

We can have all the power in the world, but if we ignore the authority we have been given to put it to work in our life ...then it's pretty much useless.

I think of it like a wrestling match. You have a couple of three hundred pound fighters in the ring who are ready to rip each other to shreds. They've trained hard, eaten right, hit the gym and have all the *power* to beat each other to a pulp. However, they can't do anything with that power until the referee, who has all the *authority* gives them the green light.

Even though the fighters are bigger, stronger and more intimidating, their power is useless without the proper authority to set it all in motion. Their fight can't even start without the right authority ...and neither can ours!

This is where many people fall short. They might be aware of the power the Bible tells us we have over Satan, but their authority to enforce it is weak and could use some work.

This is what the enemy counts on. He doesn't care if we are aware of our power over him...as long as we never feel authoritative enough to enforce it.

John 10:10 (ESV) warns us, *"The thief comes only to steal, kill and destroy."* How many times do we *let* the enemy rob us of our peace, steal our joy and use our own thoughts against us ...without ever attempting to use our God-given authority to put him in his place?

Anyone with a Bible can open it up and read about how much power we have over the devil; it's our authority we need to work on strengthening in order to really show him whose boss!

The word "authority" is defined as *"the power to give orders or make decisions: the power or right to direct or control someone or something"* (Merriam-Webster).

As Christians, we have authority over many things in our life. We have authority over how we allow ourselves to be treated, what we allow into our lives, what we will and won't put up with and even what thoughts we choose to focus on. We have the authority to command Satan to stay out of our way and the authority to control our attitudes, words and actions. The Bible is full of scriptures that reassure us of the power and authority The Holy Spirit gives us over these things. I have entire chapters dedicated to some of those topics right in this book.

1 John 3:8(NIV) even goes so far as to tell us, *"The reason the Son of God appeared was to destroy the devil's work."* Hebrews 2:14(NLT) tells us, *"Because God's children are human beings--made of flesh and blood-- the Son also became flesh and blood. For only as a human being could he die, and only by dying could he break the power of the devil, who had the power of death."* And, Colossians 2:15 tells us that Jesus has *"disarmed principalities and powers, making a public spectacle of them."* The fact that the enemy has no authority over us or our lives is made very clear throughout the Bible.

So …what seems to be the problem? The Bible tells us that God has already defeated the devil. So, why do most people, especially Christians, find themselves locked in an ongoing battle with an enemy who is already defeated and has absolutely *no authority* in our lives?

The answer is simple. Most of us do not make it a habit to regularly exercise the authority we have been given to keep Satan in his place. Even worse, there are times when we hand it right over to him on a silver platter! The enemy may have power, but he has absolutely no authority to use it in our lives …unless we give it to him!

How much sense does it make to hand over the keys to your house to a thief who wants to steal, kill and destroy everything in it? You may be thinking, … *"Well, who in their right mind would do something like that?"* The short answer is … we all do.

We do it every day in a thousand different ways. Every time we put one ounce of energy into believing the lies the devil tries to tell us, getting caught up in the confusion he tries to bring to our doorstep or entertaining the people he uses to work through, we hand more of our authority over to him.

1 Peter 5:8 (NIV) tells us to, *"Be alert and of sober mind. Your enemy the devil prowls around like a roaring lion looking for someone to devour."*

However, John 8:44 also reminds us that the devil is a liar and *"the father of all lies."* So, when the devil starts to lie to you and prowl around *pretending* to be a roaring lion … ask yourself these questions:

- *How much of my authority do I surrender to him?*
- *How quickly do I feed into his foolishness and allow him into my life?*
- *How much free reign do I give him to come in, get comfortable and wreak havoc?*

Are you like that policeman who never gets out of the car to exercise his authority and use the power he has been given to bring things to an end? Are you like those wrestlers with all the power but who lack the right authority to put it in motion? If the answer is "yes" to either of those questions…don't worry. It happens to us all.

I want to share a story with you that shows just how easy it is to surrender our authority without even realizing it and let the enemy torment us.

As I have mentioned several times, this is the first book that I've written. It was a huge amount of work and I really had no idea how much I was biting off when I got started. As I learned more about being an author, the publishing industry and how it all works, I started to become overwhelmed.

I became obsessed with deadlines, trying to secure a literary agent, writing a book proposal, building a website and increasing my presence on social media. I was stressed out, aggravated and borderline depressed at the thought of all the work that was on my plate. I was focusing so much on my work that I had stopped making music and performing with my group, which used to be a huge stress reliever. I rarely saw friends, went out to relax and have a good time and was enjoying very little in life.

I had become so focused on writing a book about God and helping other people learn how to strengthen their spirituality…that I had forgotten to make time to strengthen my own! My life was completely out of balance.

Little did I know, this was an open door for the enemy to attack. It seemed like I was always fighting negative thoughts of failure. I was angry at the thought of not having a personal life or time for myself. I had a short fuse, was easily aggravated and was even becoming resentful of my goals. I started to feel like a prisoner of my own ambition.

I knew something wasn't right and this wasn't the way God wanted me to live. I knew He wouldn't speak to me and give me the idea to write such a powerful book and then have me miserable and stressed out every step of the way. However, I chalked it up to being overworked and continued to live this way for quite some time. I even had to go back and read the chapters I wrote on the power of positivity and watching your words!

Though, it wasn't until I started doing research for this chapter that I realized what I had actually done was surrender my authority to the enemy. Even though I had the authority to put him in his place and the power to keep him there, I had handed it all over to him on a silver platter.

I had allowed him to move into my life, my thoughts, my attitude and outlook. It was like living with a noisy, relentless, ruthless, evil roommate who is doing everything he can to tear you down. And, I had handed him the keys and let him move right in!

I couldn't even get to the point of exercising my power to drive him out because I was worn out mentally! Does any of this sound familiar? This is how the enemy operates and how easily he can trick people into surrendering their authority.

However, just like everything else in this book, writing this chapter helped me tremendously! Learning some of the things I am sharing with you all in this chapter helped me take back my authority and use the power of the Holy Spirit to pack the enemy's bags and kick them to the curb!

There are millions of people who live this way everyday. It happens to everyone, from the strongest Christian to the new believer. The enemy knows our insecurities, our weaknesses and what triggers us and sends us over the edge.

It makes it so easy for him to sneak into our life and set up shop that, oftentimes, we don't even question his presence. To many people, living under his lies and torment just becomes normal.

However, there are many things we can do to strengthen our authority and become stronger at enforcing the power we have been given over the devil.

The first thing I want to talk about is improving our stance. You might be wondering what I mean by that. Well, everything from our posture, to the way we walk, speak and carry ourselves, to the words that come out of our mouth makes a huge difference in whether we appear to the enemy as a powerful force or an easy target.

I know everyone reading this has seen those National Geographic specials where a lion is shown stalking it's prey. Very rarely does the lion target the strongest, fastest, most powerful gazelle. They are always shown trailing the ones who are lagging behind, not paying attention and who appear to be the slowest and weakest.

So, ask yourself this; when the enemy prowls around *pretending* to be a roaring lion…what does he see you as? Are you someone that he doesn't want to wrestle with or are you someone that he knows he can take down easily? Do you have an authoritative stance or are you lagging behind and not paying attention?

Something as simple as walking with our shoulders back and our heads held high can do a lot to help us get in touch with our God-given authority. It can make a difference in the way the enemy sees us, how we feel about ourselves and how we appear to the world.

Imagine this; you want to get some work done on your home. You interview two contractors. The first one shuffles in with his head down, shoulders slumped, screws falling out of his tool belt and hands you a crumpled up business card. When you ask him questions about the renovation, he doesn't look you in the eye, mumbles replies, scratches his head and says things like, "I reckon" and "I guess I can do that." He doesn't come across as having the authority to hammer in a nail… much less knock down a wall.

The second one walks in with his shoulders back, head up, a clean uniform and shows you his website with samples of his work. When you ask him questions about the renovation he replies in a confident tone things like, "I sure can" and "Let me explain how I'll do that." He's assertive, confident and secure in his ability to get the job done. He comes across as being able to handle any situation that may arise. Which one would you hire?

In order to have victory over Satan, we need to be like that second contractor. It's crucial that we understand how important our stance is. There is absolutely no way we can properly exercise our authority and walk in enough power to defeat the enemy if we don't carry ourselves in an authoritative way.

I'm sure everyone reading this knows of a person who has a weak stance. When you ask them how they're doing, they reply with, "Well, I'm making it" or "…I'm here." They walk around with their head down, beaten up by life and a "just trying to make it till Jesus comes back" attitude. They don't have a commanding presence, aren't confident and don't have enough fight in them to swat a fly. This is the type of person the enemy knows is an easy target.

We have to remember, it's called spiritual *warfare* for a reason. We are at war with an enemy who will stop at nothing to destroy us. Therefore, we need to have to have a warrior's stance and carry ourselves like soldiers if we plan to win!

We have to be:

- ❖ *Commanding* instead of cowardly!
- ❖ *Powerful* instead of pitiful!
- ❖ And *Mighty* instead of mild!

I know it may be hard to live every minute of every day in that mindset. We have things in our life we have to deal with, everyday problems that challenge us and are sometimes pulled in a hundred different directions. We have all been there. So, how else can we maintain an attitude of authority in our everyday life?

Well, another good way to get in touch with our authority is to try living according to *who* the Bible tells us we are instead of *how* life makes us feel. I'll explain what I mean by that.

As human beings, our emotions will always take us on a wild roller coaster ride. We can be up one minute and down the next. We all have times in our life where we don't feel very powerful, authoritative or formidable. The enemy knows this and therefore is able to use those emotions against us. If we make it a habit to live according to how we feel, we are in for a very bumpy ride!

To overcome this and begin to walk more in our authority, we have to lean on scriptures that remind us *who* we are, despite *how* we may be feeling at the moment.

- ❖ Romans 8:37(ESV) tells us, *"No, in all these things we are more than conquerors through him who loved us."*
- ❖ Ephesians 2:10 (NLT) reminds us, *"For we are God's masterpiece. He has created us anew in Christ Jesus, so we can do the good things he planned for us long ago."*
- ❖ 2 Corinthians 4:8 (NLT) assures us that, *"We are pressed on every side by troubles, but we are not crushed. We are perplexed, but not driven to despair."*
- ❖ 1 Peter 2:9 (NIV) lets us know, *"But you are a chosen people, a royal priesthood, a holy nation, God's special possession, that you may declare the praises of him who called you out of darkness into his wonderful light."*
- ❖ And Ephesians 6:10 (NIV) tells us, *"Finally, be strong in the Lord and in his mighty power."*

Oftentimes, life has a tendency to beat us up and make us forget who we are. This is something the enemy counts on. Leaning on scriptures like these is the only way to help us remember that we are God's children and all the power and authority that comes along with that.

When the enemy attacks us and makes it hard to maintain an attitude of authority, we need to learn to go on "auto-pilot" and let scriptures like these push us forward and be the motivation to fight back!

If we make it a habit to meditate on scriptures that reinforce how we are *more than conquerors*, how we are each *God's masterpieces*, His *chosen people* and a *royal priesthood*, it'll be pretty hard *not* to have an attitude of authority!

Pretty soon, when the devil tries to come against you, no matter how you feel, your automatic response will become, "Go bother someone else…don't you know who I am??"

It might take some time, but the more you practice doing this, the easier it will become to put him in his place!

If we do this enough, it will become easier to push past how we feel and live life as the conquerors Christ gives us the power to be.

- ❖ Instead of victims…we will become *Victors*.
- ❖ Instead of whiners, we will become *Winners*.
- ❖ And, instead of weak …we will become *Warriors*!

Making it a habit to do these sorts of things helps us stay on guard and ensures that we stay one step ahead of the devil and his schemes.

Too many people, including Christians, tend to live in a passive way. We have to stop allowing the enemy time to lurk around, look for an opening and plan his attack. We have to learn to live aggressively, actively walk in our authority and cut him off at the knees!

It may not be such a nice thing to do in the business world, but when it comes to Satan…it's okay to throw our weight around and let him know whose boss! The story is already written and the devil has been defeated. However, it's up to us to use the "Power and Authority" God has given us to make sure he stays that way!

CHAPTER 12

THE FULL ARMOR

"Therefore put on the full armor of God, so that when the day of evil comes, you may be able to stand your ground, and after you have done everything, to stand. Stand firm then, with the belt of truth buckled around your waist, with the breastplate of righteousness in place, and with your feet fitted with the readiness that comes from the gospel of peace. In addition to all this, take up the shield of faith, with which you can extinguish all the flaming arrows of the evil one. Take the helmet of salvation and the sword of the Spirit, which is the word of God. And pray in the Spirit on all occasions with all kinds of prayers and requests. With this in mind, be alert and always keep on praying for all the Lord's people" (Ephesians 6:13-18, NIV).

Anyone who knows me knows that I am a huge comic book fan. I've been collecting them since I was little. I love MARVEL, DC and anything that has to do with the X-Men. Not too long ago, I watched an animated movie where Batman comes up with a plan to take out each of his fellow members of the Justice League. He came up with strategic attacks against Superman, Wonder-Woman and the Flash, which would render them defenseless in case they ever turned evil, switched sides or posed any sort of threat to mankind.

Even though he risked his life and fought beside these heroes every day, he wanted to make sure he was well prepared just in case he ever had to go toe to toe against them. In the movie, someone steals the plans

Batman came up with and begins attacking each of the heroes and he is the only one who can save them.

It was a pretty cool movie and got me thinking about the concept of being prepared. I began to think, *"What if we applied that same strategy in our fight against the devil?"* What if we devised a plan to make sure we're prepared, not *if,* but *when* Satan starts to attack us?

In the last chapter, I talked about the power we have over the devil and the authority we have been given to put it to use in our lives. I shared ways to strengthen that authority and walk in it more abundantly. At the end of that chapter, I let you know that it's okay to throw your weight around when it comes to the devil. It's the only way to make sure he stays in his place!

However, most people only attempt to do this *after* he starts attacking them. By then, it may already be too late. I shared a story of how the enemy tricked me into handing over all my authority to him. I talked about how miserable, on edge, aggravated and negative I had become. I talked about how hard I had to work to take back my authority and use it to send him packing.

After watching the movie, I couldn't help but think that maybe that situation could have been avoided if I had been better prepared for battle.

In this chapter, "The Full Armor" I want to talk about ways to make sure we're ready in our fight against Satan. I want to share strategies to make sure he has very little opening to come into our lives and wreak havoc. I also want to take a look at some very important scriptures that spell out what we need to do to stay prepared and how we can apply those lessons to our lives today.

There's a cartoon, G.I Joe, which has the tagline *"Knowing is Half the Battle."* Yes, I'm a big kid, but it's very true. Since we know that we will *always* have to fight Satan, the more prepared we are, the better chance we have at withstanding his schemes and winning the battle.

Let's begin by looking at the scriptures from Ephesians that begin this chapter (6:10-18, NIV). This is where the Apostle Paul gives us some very good advice on staying prepared for our fight against the devil.

Paul, (also known as Saul of Tarsus) was not one of the original twelve disciples of Jesus. In fact, his early life was dedicated to the persecution of the disciples in Jerusalem. It wasn't until he had a vision of the newly resurrected Jesus while traveling that he converted from Judaism to Christianity.

After his encounter with Jesus, Paul became a believer and went on to preach and declare Jesus as the Messiah and Son of God. He made several mission trips throughout the Roman Empire, established churches and played a huge part in teaching the gospel of Christ in the first century.

However, after being accused of inciting rebellions, he was imprisoned in Rome for two years. While spending time under the guard of the Roman soldiers, Paul began to draw similarities between the armor worn by his captors and the "armor" we need to wear as Christians.

In his letter to the Ephesians, Paul instructs the church on how to put on the full "armor" of God so they can be prepared to withstand the devil. As with any armor, we need to learn to put it on *before* we go into battle, not during or after. If we wait until then to scramble to protect ourselves, the devil already has the upper hand.

If we take Pauls' advice on staying prepared, we will always be ready when the enemy strikes. At the first sign of him lurking around, we will be ready to fight back and send him running in the other direction!

Let's take a look at the pieces of "armor" Paul tells us to put on and how they are an important part of spiritual warfare in our everyday life.

THE BELT OF TRUTH

Paul begins instructing us how to put on our first piece of armor in Ephesians 6:14 (NIV) by saying, *"Stand firm then, with the belt of truth buckled around your waist..."* With all the other dangerous weapons he could have chosen, it may seem odd that the first thing he tells us to put on in order to protect ourselves against the devil ...is a belt. However, once we take a closer look, it begins to make sense.

In ancient times, the belt was a very important part of a soldier's armor. It was used to hold swords, ropes, pouches and other weapons. It was tied in several places to make sure that no matter how much the soldier twisted, turned and fought …it would never come off.

Today, our belts serve a similar purpose, they are meant to hold something up or keep something in place.

When Paul tells us to keep the belt of truth buckled around our waist, I believe he is telling us to let the truth of God's Word *hold us up* in battle.

God's Word should always be the first thing we use to strike back against the devil. It should help hold our lives in place no matter what the enemy tries to throw at us. When the devil comes against us, we need to stand firm in the truth of God's Word and immediately wrap it around us tightly, just like we would a belt.

In John 8:31-32(NLT), Jesus told the people who believed in him, *"You are truly my disciples if you remain faithful to my teachings. And you will know the truth, and the truth will set you free."*

When the devil tries to attack our thoughts and tell us that we're not good enough, that we can't have a great life, be successful, live in victory or be healed, we can't lose our perspective and be shaken by his lies. We have to fire right back with the truth of the gospel and rely on it to hold us firmly in place.

Oftentimes, knowing the truth of God's Word is enough to make us realize how ridiculous and desperate the enemy can be with his lies. When we "wrap" ourselves tightly in scriptures that tell us how much God loves us (John 3:16), how He can heal us (Psalm 107:20) and how we can have an abundant life (John 10:10) we are destroying the devils attacks and protecting ourselves with our belt of truth.

Psalm 33:4 (NLT) assures us, *"For the word of the LORD holds true, and we can trust everything he does."*

The next time the enemy tries to come against you in any way, let the *truth* be your first defense. No matter what lie the devil tries to sell you, God has a word to conquer it, tell you otherwise and give you hope. Once you know the truth, I encourage you to wrap it around you tightly just like you would a belt. Once you do…you will see how it will hold the rest of your life in place!

THE BREASTPLATE OF RIGHTEOUSNESS

Paul continues on in Ephesians 6:14 to tell us to keep our breastplate of righteousness in place. This is the second piece of armor he instructs us to put on in order to protect ourselves from the devil's schemes.

It's pretty obvious how important a metal breastplate would have been to soldiers in ancient times. It would have protected their torso from spears, arrows and swords. In doing so, it would have also covered their heart. When Paul tells us to keep our breastplate of righteousness in place, I believe he is telling us to be confident in the fact that our hearts have been made right by the righteousness of the Lord.

Oftentimes, when Satan attacks us, he tries to use our own faults and shortcomings against us. He can try to trick us into thinking God could never approve of us, love us or have a relationship with us. He will use the things in our life that we need to work on to try and make us feel guilty and unworthy of God's love. Too often, this leads people to believe they have to stay away from God until they get their messes sorted out.

There are countless people walking around every day who feel like God is mad at them for some reason or another. So much so, that I dedicated the entire first section of this book to telling people otherwise!

If people don't understand that God knows their heart, they may feel guilty and try to put as much distance as they can between themselves and the Creator. This is just what the devil wants! I have seen it happen with my own eyes.

By telling us to keep our breastplate of righteousness firmly in place, Paul is telling us that, no matter how the devil tries to make us feel…we have to be *confident* that God loves us. Jesus died so we wouldn't have to feel condemned and we have to stand strong when the devil tries to make us believe different!

By keeping our breastplate of righteousness *firmly* in place, we are telling the enemy, "Yes, I know I'm not perfect, but I have been forgiven and my heart has been made right by the one who is!"

Also, the breastplate was designed to protect soldiers against head on attacks. This means when the devil tries to use our shortcomings against us, we need to stand firm and face him. We don't have to run from him and we certainly can't allow him to convince us to run from God!

2 Corinthians 5:21 (NLT) tells us, *"For God made Christ, who never sinned, to be the offering for our sin, so that we could be made right with God through Christ."*

Also, 1 Samuel 16:7 (NIV) let us know, *"The Lord does not look at the things people look at. People look at the outward appearance, but the LORD looks at the heart."*

By keeping our breastplate of righteousness firmly in place, we are making sure that Satan can no longer jab, stab or poke us with our flaws or shortcomings. He can no longer use that trick against us because we know we have been forgiven and the Lord knows our heart.

THE SHOES OF PEACE

Paul goes on in Ephesians 6:15 to tell us to make sure our feet are fitted with the readiness that comes from the gospel of peace. As anyone who has watched a boxing match or mixed martial arts fight will tell you, a good solid footing is very important. It gives us an advantage in a fight. It is even said that the Roman soldiers had footwear with spikes on the bottom to give them a strong stance and help them keep their balance.

If we take Paul's advice and apply it to our lives today, it means we should do everything we can to stay grounded in peace. If our lives are grounded in peace, we will always have a solid foundation to stand on and fight.

A solid foundation is very important. If our lives are a mess, we can be easily knocked down and defeated. I'm sure everyone reading this knows someone who is standing on a rocky foundation. I bet every time you talk to them, they are up in arms about something. Many times, it's probably something they have gotten themselves into. You may have even thought this to yourself when talking to them.

For example, I have a friend who is always worried about his finances. Now, this is something we all struggle with in one way or another. However, bill collectors are constantly hounding him for bills he let pile up over the years. Even though he has a good job and makes enough money to pay them, he spends it on other things.

He is always worried that collection agencies will catch up to him and garnish his wages for broken leases or repossessed cars. He is anxious and paranoid every time he gets a notice in the mail or a phone call from an unknown number. The devil knows this and is able to use it to steal his peace. However, if he had solid ground to stand on concerning his finances, the devil wouldn't be able to use it to attack him. This is just one example of how the devil can use our lives against us if we don't have them grounded in peace.

I used to have a neighbor who was in a bad relationship. It didn't take much to spark a late night screaming match between her and her boyfriend, which could be heard by everyone in the building. This happened so often that it resulted in her getting an eviction notice.

She came to each of the neighbors and pleaded with us to speak to the rental office on her behalf. She said she was worried and stressed because she didn't have anywhere else to go. However, if she had made it a requirement to have peace in her home and relationship, she might not have found herself in that predicament.

I have another friend who is dating more than one girl…even though they both think he is exclusively with them. He is always dodging phone calls, trying to remember what lie he told to which one and arguing with one or the other. The devil sees he is standing on rocky ground with his relationships and is able to use it to make him miserable. He told me the other day that he was ready to call it quits with both of them just to have some peace in his life.

These are just a few examples of how standing on rocky ground can make it very easy for the devil to shake us up. We have to try our best to walk in peace and not to give him any opening to attack us. Once we do, it can be like a domino effect and have an impact on many areas of our life.

Psalm 34:14 (NLT) advises us to, *"Turn away from evil and do good. Search for peace, and work to maintain it."*

To *search* for peace means we have to go out of our way to obtain it. This means we may have to stay away from certain situations, people or anything else that may jeopardize our solid foundation. It's up to us to decide how far we're willing to go to make peace a priority.

In a previous section of the book, I talked about the harmful effects negative people have on our peace of mind. I talked about how the enemy can work through those people and use their words and actions as a way to attack us. If we make walking in peace a priority, we may have to learn to make some very difficult decisions concerning people.

For example, a friend of mine recently had a situation where one of his family members caused some major drama in his otherwise peaceful family. He told me this relative said some pretty hurtful things to him and several other members of his family as well. My friend told me it wasn't the first time something like this has happened. He said this particular relative is always negative, causes confusion and has even broken up relationships between other family members.

He said in the days following the incident, he wasn't able to concentrate at work, enjoy time with his kids or barely even eat. In other words, his peaceful foundation had been shaken and he was losing ground to the enemy… all because of one person! Feeling as though this was something he couldn't allow, he took steps to correct it and protect his peace.

He said as difficult as it was, he changed his phone number and cut off all ties with this particular family member. He made sure to tell me he held no ill will or grudges against this relative. However, he could not allow the enemy to continue to work through this person to steal his peace.

This may seem drastic, but it is exactly the type of thing we have to do in order to maintain our solid foundation. Satan can take ruthless measures when trying to attack our peace and we have to be just as aggressive in defending it! Continuing to allow certain things in our life is like rolling out the welcome mat for the devil to stomp all over us.

Another way to maintain a solid, peaceful foundation is one that many people may overlook… getting enough rest.

One of my good friends came to me recently and told me how burned out he was. He said his job was causing him to be constantly on edge. He told me how the devil was taking advantage of his stressful workload and using it to make him anxious, aggravated and negative in almost every other area of his life.

He went on to say that it had been a very long time since he took some time for himself and rested. Even though he is the manager at his job, he said he was too paranoid to take the vacation time he had earned. He said the thought of getting a ton of phone calls and e-mails from his employees while trying to relax made it not even worth the effort.

Because of this, the devil had him going in circles, exhausted mentally and feeling bad physically. I shared with him the same story I shared earlier of how I was working on this book non-stop without taking the proper time to rest and recharge. I told him how I ended up feeling the same way he was feeling, until I decided to do something about it.

When we start to feel negative, tired, aggravated and burned out … that is the perfect time for the devil to attack. If we are exhausted physically and mentally, our foundation is weak and we will begin to crumble. The devil sees this and will take advantage of it as his time to pounce.

We have to remember that rest is a powerful form of spiritual warfare in helping us maintain peace. Psalm 127:2(NLT) tells us, *"It is useless for you to work so hard from early morning until late at night, anxiously working for food to eat; for God gives rest to his loved ones."*

I encouraged my friend to take a much-needed couple of days off and recharge in order to regain his solid, peaceful foundation. Making up our minds to do whatever it takes to walk in peace is a very powerful way to stay prepared against the devil's attacks!

THE SHIELD OF FAITH

Next, Paul talks to us about the shield of faith. In Ephesians 6:16(NIV), He tells us, *"In addition to all this, take up the shield of faith, with which you can extinguish all the flaming arrows of the evil one."* This is a perfect way to describe how the enemy works. Many times in life, it seems like we have to deal with one thing after another. We all have times where it feels like the devil has taken aim at us and is firing arrow after arrow.

What the apostle Paul is telling us to do in these times is to take cover behind our faith and let it shield us. In ancient times, the Roman soldiers had shields that would cover almost their entire body. They could crouch down behind them, hold them up to prevent overhead attacks and could even use them to knock down their opponent.

The more we learn to let our faith protect us in the same way, the less effect the devils "arrows" will have on us. In Biblical times, the shield was even strapped to the soldiers forearm so they would never lose it in battle. The tighter we keep our shield of faith "strapped" to us, the better we become at deflecting the enemy's attacks.

If you practice this enough, pretty soon, some of the tricks the devil once used against you may not even work anymore!

For example, I've spoken several times throughout this book about how the enemy would fire arrows at me concerning the outcome of this project. He would take aim at me and fire something like, "You've spent years working on this book and you don't even know if anyone will buy it."

I would feel the sting of that arrow and he would pull back and fire again, "You'll never get to where you want to be in life." He would finish off his attack with something like, "You've wasted all this time and probably haven't even found what you really should be doing with your life."

After a few battles like that, I learned to hold my shield of faith a little higher. Now, when he tries to fire those same old arrows, I have learned to deflect them with scriptures like, *"I have fought the good fight, I have finished the race, and I have remained faithful"*, (2 Timothy

4:7, NLT) and *"all things work together for good, for those who are called according to his purpose"* (Romans 8:28, ESV).

We have to learn to use our shield of faith to block everything the enemy tries to throw at us. When he tries to convince us that our needs can't be met, we have to be *shielded* by scriptures like Mark 11:24 (NIV) which says, *"Therefore I tell you, whatever you ask for in prayer, believe that you have received it, and it will be yours."*

When he tries to convince us that we can't make it through trials and tribulations, we have to *hold up* scriptures like James 1:3(NIV) that declares, *"Because you know that the testing of your faith produces perseverance."*

When he tries to tell us that we can't live in abundance, we have to *take cover* behind scriptures like John 6:35(NIV) which says, *"Then Jesus declared, 'I am the bread of life. Whoever comes to me will never go hungry, and whoever believes in me will never be thirsty."*

When he tries to come against us with sickness, we have to use our shield of faith to *knock him down* with scriptures like James 5:15(KJV) which assures us, *"And the prayer of faith shall save the sick, and the Lord shall raise him up; and if he have committed sins, they shall be forgiven him."*

We have to use our shield of faith to beat him over the head every chance we get! Eventually, the devil will get so tired of hearing you declare the faithfulness of the Lord over everything, that he will turn around and retreat!

However, the shield of faith also serves a double purpose. Many of you may be familiar with the term "the best defense is a good offense". You may have heard it in a movie or read it in a book somewhere. It has been used when coming up with military strategies, sports plays and even in business. It has helped soldiers, top athletes and the most successful executives stay ahead of their competition.

It means if you can take your opponent out before *he* tries to take *you* out, he'll be so busy fending off your attack that he won't be able to mount any sort of counterattack.

Well, our shield of faith can also be used as an offensive weapon. We don't have to wait for the enemy to attack us before we decide to put it up to defend ourselves. We can use our shield of faith anytime we want to help us propel forward through life!

Much like the Roman army, who would form a line with their shields held high to storm an enemy barricade, we can hold up our shield and knock down anything that stands in our way! We can use it to topple fear, hesitation and doubt. We can use it to plow through any obstacles, roadblocks or barricades. And, we can use it to push ourselves forward towards the things we want in life.

We can use our shield of faith to ask for that promotion we feel like we've worked hard for, to make that big move we may be considering or to follow the dream that's in our heart.

I'm sure everyone reading this is familiar with 2 Corinthians 5:7, which tells us to walk by faith and not by sight. Well, I challenge you to do just that and speak faith over everything you do.

In ancient times, a soldier's shield often had a crest or an emblem on it, which symbolized which army they were in. They did this so that soldiers fighting in close combat situations wouldn't get confused and attack someone in their own battalion. When we hold up our shields, we have to remember that they bear the name of Jesus Christ! Philippians 2:10 tells us that His name is above all others and upon hearing it every knee in Heaven, on Earth and under Earth shall bow.

If we live by our faith in God, we won't even have to *slow down* when the devil comes against us. We can just hold up our shield, knock him aside and plow full steam ahead through the battlefield of life!

THE HELMET OF SALVATION

The next piece of armor Paul tells us to put on is our helmet of salvation. The Roman army had some of the most elaborate helmets of their time. They were bronze or brushed metal. They had a leather lining, chinstraps, a visor and a ridge on top for plumage or brush, depending on a soldiers rank.

Being that they went to such elaborate means to protect their heads from injury, Paul compares it to how vigilant we have be to protect what goes on in our mind.

As you have learned by now, our mind is the devil's favorite playground. If he can defeat us there ...he will win. This means we should put on our "helmet" of salvation to protect our thoughts and become mindful of what influences we allow in.

Now, here's the tricky part. This can mean different things to different people. What you may consider a "threat" to your salvation, others may not.

For example, I have an offbeat sense of humor, I like horror movies, I have tattoos, I enjoy a margarita or glass of wine and I'm in a rap group that isn't necessarily PG-13. Even though I don't consider any of these things a threat to my salvation, certain people may view it as offensive to theirs. I completely understand that.

However, there are things that I view as an absolute threat to my salvation that some of those same people may be totally fine with. For instance, I can't stand gossiping, complaining or negativity. I don't like pretentious, phony people or people who view themselves as more important than others. Those are the types of things that offend my salvation.

I mentioned a few chapters ago that I know certain people, even Christians, who thrive off those sorts of things. Everyone is different.

For example, there here have been times where co-workers, friends or family members have been speaking negatively about one thing or another. In those situations, I knew I had to put on my helmet of salvation to protect my own thoughts. If I didn't, I knew I ran the risk of being influenced by their words, mood and energy. I either chose to speak up, stay quiet or remove myself from the conversation altogether.

When I wake up in the morning, one of the first things I do is turn on the TV. However, if there is a court show or talk show on where people are arguing loudly or fussing back and forth...I can't change the channel fast enough. I refuse to start my day by listening to people argue and fuss over stupid things.

On the other hand, there are people who love their morning routine of having a cup of coffee while watching Judge Judy or The View. Even my grandmother loves watching the chaos on the Jerry Springer show!

RIGHTEOUSNESS, THE REMIX- TURN UP THE VOLUME ON GOD!

The point is, you have to decide for *yourself* what is and what isn't a threat to *your* salvation. What's even more important is realizing that what offends you …someone else may be completely fine with. We have every right to protect our salvation against what offends us. However, if we offend others in the process…we really haven't accomplished much.

This reminds me of a story my buddy told me about his mom. I have been friends with this guy for a long time and have met his mom several times over the years. She is a Christian woman and a very sweet lady. However, he says it's become a chore spending time with her because she is offended by *everything.*

He told me his family tries to get together at least once a week to have dinner and enjoy each other's company. However, during those family nights, he says his mom almost runs herself ragged.

If they're watching a TV show, she gets up and leaves the room every time the commercials come on because they may advertise beer or show someone kissing. He said when him or his brother makes a joke about anything… she gets upset and walks away. He says they can't even play cards when they get together because it will offend her.

Even though he was laughing when he told me, he says it's become a huge problem at family gatherings like Thanksgiving and Christmas. He said even though she's there…she's hardly around!

He said she even gets offended at church! Apparently, there was a youth program where the young people were putting on a show. He said his cousin, who is about twelve or so, decided to sing in the program. He said his mom was excited about the performance.

However, when the little girl decided to sing over a beat from a popular song that plays on the radio and change the lyrics to sing about The Lord…his mom got offended. He said right in the middle of the child's performance, his mom got up from her seat in the first row and walked out. Imagine how that kid must have felt!

My point in telling that story is that we have to be mindful of how we go about wearing our helmet of salvation. There are ways to stand up for what we believe in without putting others down or making them feel bad in the process.

Yes, there are times when something you don't agree with presents such a huge threat that you have to do something about it right then and there. However, every situation isn't a "run for your life" scenario.

Jesus stood firm for what He believed in while making others want to be a part of it at the same time.

Ephesians 4:14(NLT) tells us, *"Then we will no longer be immature like children. We won't be tossed and blown about by every wind of new teaching. We will not be influenced when people try to trick us with lies so clever they sound like the truth."*

Even though there are times when we have to put on our helmet of salvation to protect our thoughts against what may offend us, we can't strap it on so tight that we cut off circulation to our brain!

My favorite preacher, Joyce Meyer likes to say, "The scripture says we are to have our minds renewed...not *removed*!"

In one her conferences, she even said one of her younger sons came to her and told her that she might want to take a closer look at some of the things she gets offended by. She said once she really thought about it, she realized she is okay with wearing jeans in her meetings, having a rock band play worship music onstage and changing to keep up with the times.

We are certainly living in a very different world than Paul was when he wrote this passage. There are changes taking place in the way people think, live, worship, love and even raise families. We have every right to put on our helmet of salvation to protect ourselves against things that may offend our spirit. However, just remember not to pull it down so far that it covers your eyes and causes you to stumble over every little thing!

THE SWORD OF THE SPIRIT

Paul continues on in Ephesians 6:17 to tell us about the last piece of armor we need to put on to stay prepared against the devil's attacks… the sword of the spirit. It's very interesting that Paul chose the sword to describe the Word of God.

In ancient times, soldiers used their swords for everything. They used them to cook, to split wood, cut rope and of course take down their enemies. It was a weapon for all occasions, just like God's Word!

I believe one reason Paul chose the sword to describe the Word of God is to show us that it is a practical tool for every area of our lives. As I will explore in the next section of the book, there is no area of our lives the enemy can attack that God's Word doesn't already have covered.

Just like a real sword, we can use His word to cut straight to the core of the enemy's deceit and expose the truth.

Hebrews 4:12(ISV) tells us, *"For the word of God is living and active, sharper than any double-edged sword, piercing until it divides soul and spirit, joints and marrow, as it judges the thoughts and purposes of the heart."*

However, the power of God's Word can only work for us if we put it to use in our lives! Many times, people fall victim to the enemy's lies and spend their entire life in bondage, just because they don't use their sword to fight back.

In the Bible, we have an arsenal of truth, knowledge, wisdom, power and hope right at our fingertips…and some people never even bother to use it. There's no way we can expect to have victory in our lives if we ignore the very words that tell us how to go about getting it!

Psalm 119:130 tells us, *"The unfolding of your words gives light; it gives understanding to the simple."* Psalm 119:105 also assures us that God's Word is a *"lamp for our feet and light on our path."* Once we understand how powerful it is, we can let it lead us through everything in life.

Much like the shield of faith, the sword of the spirit is an offensive weapon. Of course we can use it to defend ourselves when the enemy starts to attack us, but why wait?

No matter what we're going through in life, how we feel or what we have to overcome, the Word of God is ready and able to strike on our behalf! If we speak it and believe it, we are destroying the enemy's attack before he can even launch it. This is a surefire way to keep him at bay!

Another reason I believe Paul describes God's Word as "the sword of the spirit" is because that's where certain scriptures speak to us… deep down in our *spirit*.

We have to remember, the Bible was written over a period of about two thousand years, by forty different authors, some who spoke different languages. It has been translated into about five hundred languages, has been influenced by Kings (King James commissioned his version in the early 1600's) and intertwines faith, politics and the church.

Even though the Bible (as a whole) is a Holy and sacred book, there are certain parts that just may not speak to us the way others do. There are certain parts that may not be as relevant in helping us live abundant, victorious lives *today* as it did back *then*. We have to use our spirit to discern the difference.

There are some pretty strange scriptures in the Bible, such as Leviticus 19:19 (NASB), which warns us, *"You shall not breed together two kinds of your cattle; you shall not sow your field with two kinds of seed, nor wear a garment upon you of two kinds of material mixed together"*

There's also Leviticus 19:27(NLT) which says, *"Do not trim off the hair on your temples or trim your beards."* Those types of scriptures may have held a greater importance for people back then than they do today.

There are also scriptures in the Bible that say women should remain silent in church (1Corinthians, 14:34-35), that we shouldn't eat shellfish (Leviticus 11:10), that even people who divorce and remarry are guilty of adultery (Mark 10: 11-12) and that women who aren't virgins should be stoned to death (Deuteronomy 22:21). Yikes!

The Bible can be very confusing. When reading it, you have to ask yourself, *"Which scriptures are relevant to the **times** they were living in and which ones are **timeless** and still relevant to helping us live today?"*

It's the timeless scriptures such as the Ten Commandments or the ones that declare God's love for us that make as much sense *now* as they did back *then*.

You will know it when you read them because they will ring true, you will be able to relate them to your life *today* and you will feel them in your spirit. These are the ones we have to hold onto and be led by.

Paul concludes his instructions to us on putting on the full "armor" of God by telling us to pray in the spirit on *all* occasions with *all* kinds of prayers. He then urges us to stay *alert* and keep praying for all the Lord's people.

RIGHTEOUSNESS, THE REMIX- TURN UP THE VOLUME ON GOD !

Now that we have been equipped with a full arsenal of spiritual armor, we have to practice using it to be better prepared for our battle with the enemy.

I know it may seem like a lot. You may be thinking, *"How am I supposed to remember all of this?"* It may seem like a chore to get up every day and strap on the belt of truth, the breastplate of righteousness, put on your shoes of peace, grab your shield of faith, strap on your helmet of salvation and unsheathe your Sword of the spirit. You may feel weighed down just thinking about it.

However, it's nothing compared to the weight of the devil's attack if he catches you unprepared. In the animated movie I was watching, Batman prepared himself just *in case* he ever had to do battle with his allies. We, on the other hand, know *for sure* that we will always have to fight the devil. So, why wouldn't we do what's necessary to stay prepared? I mean, after all…we are smarter than a cartoon character, right?

SECTION 5
FIGHT THE FEAR!

CHAPTER 13

INSIDE THE FEAR

"For God has not given us a spirit of fear and timidity, but of power, love, and self-discipline" (2 Timothy 1:7, NLT).

In the last section of the book, we talked about spiritual warfare. We took an in-depth look at the battle going on in our mind, the enemy we're up against and learned some very powerful ways to protect ourselves against his schemes. We learned about power and authority, the importance of staying prepared and how to fight back using the full armor of God.

However, just because we are suited up for battle doesn't mean the devil is going to sit back, twiddle his thumbs or go down easily. He is a tricky, ruthless and often desperate opponent. He has no problem fighting dirty and hitting us below the belt.

He has an array of weapons, methods and tactics that have worked since the beginning of time and he is very good at deploying them.

In this chapter, "Inside the Fear", we'll take a look at how he uses one of the oldest tricks in the book against us…fear. I'll show you how the devil can use this one small emotion to turn our lives upside down, hold us back from our destiny and keep us from moving forward. I'll help you learn how to use the Sword of the Spirit, (which we learned about in the last chapter) to cut him down and push past this little four-letter word that so many people let rule their lives.

We'll also take a look at how he has been able to use this same trick against us for thousands of years and how some of the most well known people in the Bible dealt with fear.

Remember, our emotions are an awesome part of what makes us human, but when the devil begins to use them against us …it's time to get them under control and take our power back!

Let's begin by taking a look at what fear really is. In doing research for this chapter, I came across countless definitions of what it means to feel fear. Almost every explanation of fear included phrases like "a *perceived* threat" or "an unpleasant *emotion* or *belief*".

I'll skip the boring stuff about the different parts of the brain like the thalamus, hypothalamus and sensory cortex. Essentially, being afraid starts with a trigger. That trigger then sends a signal to the brain and results in our body releasing chemicals that can cause our heart to race, pulse to speed up, brow to perspire, muscles to tense and can even freeze us right in our tracks.

It's mind-blowing to think that a single thought can cause this type of reaction.

However, many things can trigger this response. It can be something non-life threatening like seeing a spider in your room or the thought of having to speak in front of a large audience. Or, it could be something more detrimental like being the victim of a crime or losing control of your automobile on an icy road. Either way, when we feel any type of fear…our bodies react the same.

As I was learning more about the subject, I realized that most of our fears fall into one of two categories

- ❖ Fear of the *obvious* and
- ❖ Fear of the *unknown*

Your car spinning out of control on an icy highway is a very *obvious* reason to feel fear. When something like that happens, the possible outcome is near certain. You could end up with a totaled car, downed trees and a banged up driver. I don't think anyone would question your reaction if, after you got it under control, your heart was still racing, you were breathing hard and sweating uncontrollably. That is a very natural response to an obviously frightening situation.

However, it's the other category …fear of the *unknown*, where the devil can really play with our mind and impact our life.

The devil often gets his kicks by taunting us with what we don't know. For example:

- Getting laid off from a job and facing financial uncertainty
- Being diagnosed with an illness
- Stepping out on a limb and using all of your savings to start a new business
- Moving to a new city where you don't know anyone and starting over

All of these can be scary things, which he can use to send our imagination into overdrive.

The enemy likes for us to ponder over situations. He likes for us to overthink things, get caught up in "what if's", weighing out negative scenarios and living out situations that haven't even happened yet. This is how he is able to get his hooks into us and make us feel afraid.

How else would being laid off from your job turn into thinking you'll end up broke, penniless and living on the street? How else would being diagnosed with a treatable and manageable illness translate to you giving up on life and planning your own funeral? And, how else would an exciting opportunity like starting a new business make you feel like a disaster and a failure…before you even get started? The answer is simple…fear.

The devil loves to lead us down paths of imaginary destruction. Unless we learn how to fight back, we had best strap on our seatbelts because life will be a very bumpy ride!

Let's begin breaking down the process the devil uses to make us feel fear.

My favorite preacher, Joyce Meyer, uses an awesome acronym for fear… it's

- ❖ **False**
- ❖ **Evidence**

- ❖ **A**ppearing
- ❖ **R**eal

The devil is a tremendous liar and a master at selling us false evidence. Once we understand that's how most of our fears originate, we are one step closer to being able to recognize them for the lies they really are. So, from here on out, I'll be using that acronym to refer to fear…just to keep the devil's false evidence in perspective!

The first thing the devil needs to launch an attack of F.E.A.R against us is …opportunity.

I'm sure many of you are familiar with the saying, "An idle mind is the devil's workshop". Well, the word *idle* means "lazy, empty and inactive".

When we come up against a situation in our lives where the outcome may be uncertain, our minds are left completely open to ponder all the possibilities. However, this means they are also left completely open to F.E.A.R as well.

If we don't take charge and purposely fill our mind with positive thoughts and focus on the promises of the Lord regarding the situation, the enemy will step in and fill them up for us!

If we have lazy thoughts that wander around aimlessly, he will fill them up with doubt, dread, trepidation and anxiety. He will keep them busy with worry, reasoning, rationalizing and agonizing. He will have us replay the worst scenarios over in our mind until we have created a mountain of F.E.A.R that we now have to try and overcome. Before you know it, our mind will go from "idle" to "overdrive"… and it will be speeding completely in the wrong direction!

No matter how good the situation may be …a new move, getting married, a new baby, a promotion or a whole new career path…if we let our minds wander around aimlessly, we are inviting the devil to turn them upside down with F.E.A.R.

Imagine this, there is a young bride who is about to get married. She's spent her whole engagement excited and looking forward to spending her life with her new husband. The plans are made, the venue is booked and the invitations have been sent out.

However, as the wedding day draws near...the more her mind begins to wander. She may ask herself things like, *"Am I making the right decision"* or *"Is he really the one for me?"*

Unless she gets her thoughts on track, the devil will step in and use this as an opportunity to magnify those doubts. She may become apprehensive, uneasy and even have second thoughts.

The wedding dress she was so excited about now makes her break out in hives at the thought of putting it on. The guest list she had trouble narrowing down now makes her wish everyone would call and cancel. And, the over the top wedding cake she wanted makes her nauseas just thinking about it.

Many people call this "cold feet" or the "jitters", but lets just keep it real and call it what it is...F.E.A.R. She is about to embark on a new life with someone else and that can be pretty scary. The devil knows this and has taken full advantage of it.

Without focusing her thoughts on the promises of the Lord and meditating on scriptures about love, like 1 Corinthians 13:4-7(ESV) which would reassure her, *"Love is patient and kind; love does not envy or boast; it is not arrogant or rude. It does not insist on its own way; it is not irritable or resentful; it does not rejoice at wrongdoing, but rejoices with the truth. Love bears all things, believes all things, hopes all things, and endures all things"* or Proverbs 3:5-6 (NLT) which would encourage her to, *"Trust in the LORD with all your heart; do not depend on your own understanding. Seek his will in all you do, and he will show you which path to take"*...she is vulnerable to any old thing the devil wants to dump in her head.

And rest assured, even though he didn't get an invitation, he *will* show up and try to use this exciting occasion against her!

This is just an example of how he can show up and try to ruin the *good* times in our life. Imagine how much more real his attacks seem when we're going through hard times or facing uncertainty over our finances, family or health! We have to stop giving the enemy the opportunity to hop in the drivers seat and send our mind careening down the path of worst possibilities!

One way to avoid falling into this trap is to do what I like to call...

- ❖ **T**hinking
- ❖ **O**n
- ❖ **P**urpose (or staying on "T.O.P" of your thoughts)

When we're facing difficult situations or an unknown future, we have to learn to *immediately* go to work and take control of our thoughts. We cannot let our minds wander. We have to deliberately focus on the positive and put more trust in what God says about the situation than any lie the devil tries to hurl at us.

1 Peter 1:13(NASB) tells us, *"Therefore, prepare your minds for action, keep sober in spirit, fix your hope completely on the grace to be brought to you at the revelation of Jesus Christ."* And, Philippians 4:8(NIV) instructs us, *"Finally, brothers and sisters, whatever is true, whatever is noble, whatever is right, whatever is pure, whatever is lovely, whatever is admirable--if anything is excellent or praiseworthy--think about such things."*

In other words, if it doesn't help you move forward, don't think about it! It may be easier said than done but remember…our thoughts are ours to control. Even though our minds may wander… which direction they wander in is completely up to us!

Staying on "T.O.P" of our thoughts gives the devil less room to work and ensures that we focus on things that will help us, not hinder us.

Another thing that will help us overcome F.E.A.R and keep it in the proper perspective is to better understand its purpose. For starters, F.E.A.R is a cheap distraction the enemy uses to hold us back. No matter how big or small the F.E.A.R is, it's designed to keep us from moving forward.

There are millions of people who are afraid of everything from flying to animals, to water, heights, germs, small spaces, doctors, needles and even failure, intimacy or commitment. Even though these F.E.A.R's are legitimate in the persons mind, I guarantee you they have done nothing to enhance their lives and have only held them back in one way or another.

For example, I have a buddy of mine who is almost thirty. He's been at the same job since he graduated high school. Even though the company has tried to promote him many times, he will only let himself go so far up the corporate ladder. He's turned down offers to be a training coordinator and even district manager because it means he will have to fly different places. He is deathly afraid of planes and has vowed never to get on one even though it's clear to him that it's holding him back in his career.

I have another friend who, for years, had a F.E.A.R of going to the dentist. He avoided teeth cleanings and routine check ups. After suffering with a horrible toothache, he had no choice but to give in and go. Now, he is faced with having to have teeth pulled and a possible root canal. The F.E.A.R he built up in his mind kept him from going to the dentist for years and possibly could have prevented what he's going through now.

I even turned down the opportunity to go on an awesome vacation with friends because it was on a cruise ship. I have a huge F.E.A.R of being stuck out in the middle of the ocean. The thought of looking around and seeing nothing but water for miles sends my imagination into a panic. I automatically picture myself clinging to a life raft with help days away!

Even though the vacation was free as an incentive from my job, all my friends were going and my ticket was already booked…I backed out at the last minute. Needless to say, my friends went, had an awesome time and enjoyed telling me how much fun I missed.

These are just a few small examples of how people let F.E.A.R hold them back every day. Some people never open themselves up to others, find love, believe they are good enough, pursue their dreams or ever leave their comfort zone…all because of F.E.A.R.

I probably would have never written one word of this book if I had listened to all my F.E.A.R's. I still have to remind myself daily that the devil would like nothing more than for me to turn around and stop moving forward.

I'm sure everyone reading this can think of at least one area where the enemy uses F.E.A.R to try and stop you from moving forward. Remember, he only wants to hold you back from the great things God has planned for your life and you can't allow him to do that!

When we feel F.E.A.R holding us back from something, it should make us more determined than *ever* to push through and see what the enemy is trying so hard to keep us from on the other side!

I'm happy to say that my buddy who was afraid of flying recently did just that. He had to attend a meeting in Canada and to get there, had to take not one plane...but two! Even though he said he was a nervous wreck the entire way, it wasn't nearly as bad as he thought it would be. He arrived in Canada and made a great impression on the new owners of the company. Now, his company wants to promote him more than ever! However, this time he may actually consider taking the position.

He told me, even though he doesn't enjoy flying, that he no longer has a F.E.A.R of it!

This is how we have to approach life. We will always feel F.E.A.R about certain things. There is nothing wrong with that. However, if we allow the devil to blow that F.E.A.R out of proportion and hold us back from moving forward ...we'll never know what we could be missing out on.

Besides using F.E.A.R to hold us back, the devil also uses it as a ploy to try and distract us from God. He wants us to be so consumed with reasoning, overthinking, rationalizing and trying to figure everything out for ourselves ...that we completely lose sight of the fact that God already has our future figured out and in His hands!

One of my favorite scriptures, which has helped me stay focused on God in the face of F.E.A.R, is Jeremiah 29:11(NIV). It assures us, *"For I know the plans I have for you," declares the LORD, "plans to prosper you and not to harm you, plans to give you hope and a future."* No matter what I've faced in life, I've leaned on that scripture harder than any of the circumstances that have come my way!

Imagine how small our F.E.A.R's would seem if we focused on the promises of God in that *one* scripture alone!

However, the enemy knows if we put our complete trust and faith in God...we will become unstoppable! So, he uses F.E.A.R to confuse us, make us second-guess ourselves, become double- minded and even doubt God's ability to provide and care for us!

He's been using the same old trick against us since the beginning of time …yet somehow, we still fall for it!

This is how he tricked Eve in the Garden of Eden. He tempted her with knowledge and scared her into believing there was something she was missing out on. She became so afraid that God was holding something back from her and Adam by not allowing them to eat from the tree of Knowledge, that she took the apple. She was confused, double minded, lost sight of God…and took a bite. And, we all know how well that ended!

Matthew 14:20-31 shows us how F.E.A.R also caused Peter to become distracted and lose sight of the Lord. Shortly after Jesus and the disciples fed a crowd of over five thousand people with only five loaves of bread and two fish, Jesus sent the disciples away and went to the mountaintop to pray by himself.

When Jesus was done, the disciples were far away from the mountain in a boat which was being whipped around by strong waves and heavy winds. Jesus decided to walk out on the water towards the boat. When the disciples saw Him they got scared and thought He was a ghost.

Matthew 14:27(NLT) says, *"But Jesus spoke to them at once. 'Don't be afraid,' he said. "Take courage. I am here!"* Matthew 14:28 (NLT) explains, *"Then Peter called to him, "Lord, if it's really you, tell me to come to you, walking on the water."*

The story goes on to tell us how Jesus did what Peter asked and called for him to walk out on the water. Peter got out of the boat and started walking towards Jesus. He was doing fine for a while …until F.E.A.R got the best of him.

Matthew 14:30-31(NLT) tells us, *"But when he saw the strong wind and the waves, he was terrified and began to sink. "Save me, Lord!" he shouted. Jesus immediately reached out and grabbed him. "You have so little faith," Jesus said. "Why did you doubt me?"*

Peter had the courage to move forward as long as he stayed focused on the Lord. However, the *minute* he took his eyes off Jesus and started paying attention to the storm around him, he got scared and began to sink. Does this sound familiar?

I'm sure many of you can relate to this story. How many times has the devil distracted you with so much F.E.A.R that you completely focused on your circumstances and took your eyes off God? Once we do this, we begin to sink just like Peter did!

The enemy used F.E.A.R to make Peter doubt the Lord's ability to take care of him in the middle of the storm. And, he does the exact same thing to us!

I'm telling you now; even in the strong wind and rough water, we can't allow the enemy to distract us and make us doubt the Lord's ability to keep us afloat!

Right now, there is someone reading this who is afraid to get out of the "boat" and walk toward Jesus. There is someone who is afraid to do something the Lord has told them to do because they are focused on the F.E.A.R the enemy is using against them.

I want to let you know; Jesus is saying the same thing to you that he told the disciples in Matthew 14:27, which is, *"Don't be afraid, Take courage. I am here!"*

Trust me, you don't want to let the devil win and hear the Lord say *"You have so little faith. Why did you doubt me?"* (Matthew 14:31, NLT) So, I encourage you to keep moving forward!

When talking about God's desire for us to move forward in the face of F.E.A.R, I like to use the story of Lot's wife.

Lot, who was Abraham's nephew, lived in Sodom with his wife and daughters. To say the city of Sodom and its neighboring city, Gomorrah were unruly, greedy, idol-worshipers would be an extreme understatement. All kinds of things were taking place in these two cities. God revealed to Abraham that He would destroy both. However, thinking of Lot, Abraham asked God if He would have mercy if there were righteous people found to live there.

God agreed and then sent two angels in the form of men to the city of Sodom to investigate. Upon entering the city, they were met by Lot. Lot showed the strangers hospitality and invited them to eat and spend the night with his family.

After dinner, however, is when things got a little sketchy. Let's just say the evening did not go smoothly once the men in the city found out that Lot had houseguest and tried to exact their own brand of supremacy (you can read the story for yourself in Genesis).

After making an escape and striking the men in the city blind, the two angels instructed Lot to take anyone who "belonged" to him and escape the city because it was going to be destroyed. After an unsuccessful attempt to convince his sons-in-law to leave, Lot grabbed his wife and his daughters and fled.

However, as they were leaving, one of the angels instructed him, *"Flee for your lives! Don't look back, and don't stop anywhere in the plain! Flee to the mountains or you will be swept away!"* (Genesis 19:17,NIV)

As they were making their way to safety, burning sulfur rained down from the sky and began to destroy the cities. For whatever reason, Lot's wife stopped to look back and was turned into a pillar of salt, (Genesis 19:26). Lot and his daughters were forced to continue their journey on their own (which also took a turn for the weird).

Many people draw their own conclusions from this. Some say she was punished for her unwillingness to let go of her old life. Some say it was a consequence for caring about her material possessions, which were being destroyed. I look at it as a result of disobeying God and not continuing to move forward in the face of F.E.A.R.

The message I take away from it is this; once God tells you to move on…move on and don't look back!

When it comes to F.E.A.R, the Bible tells us over and over again that it doesn't even have to be an issue for us.

As for a fearful attitude,

- ❖ 2 Timothy 1:7(NLT) tells us, *"For God has not given us a spirit of fear and timidity, but of power, love, and self-discipline."*

When it comes to people,

- ❖ Psalms 118:6(ESV) reminds us, *"The LORD is on my side; I will not fear. What can man do to me?"*

When we're going through difficult times,

❖ Psalms 23:4(ESV) assures us, *"Even though I walk through the valley of the shadow of death, I will fear no evil, for you are with me; your rod and your staff, they comfort me."*

When the enemy attacked me with F.E.A.R over the outcome of this book, one of my favorite scriptures to strike back with was 1 Chronicles 28:20 (NLT), where David tells Solomon *""Be strong and courageous, and do the work. Don't be afraid or discouraged, for the LORD God, my God is with you. He will not fail you or forsake you. He will see to it that all the work related to the Temple of the LORD is finished correctly."*

There are even scriptures in the Bible that speak on the F.E.A.R of love. 1 John 4:18 (ESV) tells us, *"There is no fear in love, but perfect love casts out fear. For fear has to do with punishment, and whoever fears has not been perfected in love."*

As you can see, when it comes to F.E.A.R, we have an arsenal of different scriptures that can cut it down to the core. However, many people never even bother to strike back. They just curl up in a ball and let the devil bombard their thoughts with F.E.A.R. Perhaps they don't know how to fight back or that it's even an option. Well, it is!

We have every right to stand up for ourselves and use the Sword of the Spirit to slash the enemy's lies to pieces! No matter what type of F.E.A.R the enemy throws at us, our Sword of the Spirit is more than capable of striking it down and breaking it apart. Some of us just have to take it out, sharpen the blade and start attacking!

Now that we've taken a look "Inside the Fear", hopefully you understand more about this little four- letter word that sometimes seems too big to conquer. Now that we've learned *how* and *why* the enemy uses it against us, it will be easier to keep it in its proper perspective.

Conquering F.E.A.R is always going to be a work in progress. However, if we stay on "T.O.P" of our thoughts, stay focused on the Lord and use our Sword of the Spirit to cut the enemy down; he won't have much of an opportunity to make his "**False Evidence Appear Real.**" Who knows, after I read this chapter a few more times …I may even be ready to take that cruise!

CHAPTER 14

DARE TO BELIEVE!

"Your right hand, O LORD, is glorious in power. Your right hand, O LORD, smashes the enemy" (Exodus 15:6, NLT).

Now that we have blown the lid off F.E.A.R and exposed some of the devil's tricks and tactics, I'd like for you to try something: take a minute and think about your top three F.E.A.Rs.

I'm not talking about little things that scare you once in a while like spiders or hearing a noise in the house after you've watched a scary movie. I'm talking about the things that you think about often. I'm talking about the things that, no matter how well your life may be going, are always there tugging at the back of your mind. We all have them. Some of us may not even realize it.

I bet if I conducted an experiment and asked a group of people to do the same thing, their top three F.E.A.Rs would probably be pretty similar.

We all have areas in our life that we are constantly concerned about. The devil knows this and likes to attack those areas specifically. He likes to play dirty, deliver low blows and hit us where it hurts the most. He takes pleasure in trying to turn our everyday concerns into "common F.E.A.Rs" that most of us all share.

In this chapter, "Dare to Believe!" I want to expose some of the enemy's favorite targets. I want to show you how God knew that certain parts of our life would be attacked with F.E.A.R more than others and has already given us His reassurance concerning each and every one of them. I'll share tips on how to fight back when the devil attacks the areas in our life we care about the most. We'll also talk about how to go one step beyond fighting him by learning to "Dare to Believe" in the power of God in today's crazy world.

Let me start by asking you this: have you ever experienced a period in your life where everything was going so well that you thought, *"This is too good to be true?"* Have you ever found yourself unable to fully enjoy those moments because you're sitting around waiting for "the other shoe" to drop? If you have, don't worry…you're just like a lot of people. However, most people never talk about it. If everyone who felt this way went around talking about how they're worried something bad was going to happen, they would probably look unstable, obsessive compulsive or just plain crazy. Nevertheless, it's pretty normal.

One of the devils main goals is to shatter two of the most important gifts Jesus has given us …His peace and His joy.

In John 14:27(NLT), Jesus tells us, *"I am leaving you with a gift… peace of mind and heart. And the peace I give is a gift the world cannot give. So don't be troubled or afraid."* And, Nehemiah 8:10 (NIV) tells us to, *"Go and enjoy choice food and sweet drinks, and send some to those who have nothing prepared. This day is holy to our Lord. Do not grieve, for the joy of the LORD is your strength."*

However, many people find it difficult to fully enjoy life the way the Bible instructs us to. This is because the devil is constantly trying to chip away at our peace. He has spent an eternity studying us and knows exactly how our mind works. He knows we all have areas in our life we hold dear to us, worry over and are sensitive about. It's his goal to destroy our peace by turning those normal concerns into dark clouds of F.E.A.R that follow us around constantly. And, he accomplishes that goal exceptionally well with many people.

It is estimated that 42 billion dollars a year is spent to treat anxiety disorders in the United States *alone*. In fact, anxiety disorders are the most common mental illness in the U.S, affecting 40 million adults ages eighteen and over (*National Institute of Mental Health).

That means the devil is busy making a lot of people worry about a lot of things!

As long as we allow the enemy to use the things we're concerned about against us, we won't be able to enjoy life, live it to the fullest or truly appreciate the wonderful things the Lord blesses us with. No matter if these concerns cross our mind a few times a day or cripple us with F.E.A.R, we have to learn to take control of them. Let's start looking at some of the enemy's prime targets. I'm sure they will sound pretty familiar.

OUR SAFETY

I believe one of the main areas the enemy likes to use against us is the concern we all have for our safety, the safety of our family and the safety of those close to us. It's no secret that today's world can be a pretty messed up place. We can't turn on the news without seeing story after story that causes us to shake our head in disbelief. It seems like some people have completely lost their mind.

With the increase of random violence like theatre shootings, nightclub shootings, school massacres and general psychos running rampant, it's normal for us to have a heightened sense of concern for our safety and what's going on around us.

The enemy knows this and is able to use it to his full advantage. He knows that in today's world it's pretty easy for him to blow that concern way out of proportion, even to the point of causing some people excessive F.E.A.R and anxiety. I mean really, who would have ever thought we would have to wonder if we'll make it home or not before buying a movie ticket or even going to church?

While it's necessary in the world we live in to use common sense and be conscious and aware of what's going on around us, we cannot let that concern stop us from enjoying life. Some people have let the devil scare them into doing just that!

They have such a huge F.E.A.R for their safety and that of their parents, children, husbands, wives, friends and other relatives that it distracts them from enjoying life and completely overshadows God's ability to protect us.

They may do things like:

- Refuse to get on a plane
- Stay away from crowds
- Are afraid to drive on the interstate
- Won't visit certain places in the world
- Have to be home by a particular time at night or even
- Stay away from certain people

All of this is because the devil has turned their concern into F.E.A.R. However, the Lord has left us reassurance of His strength and protection all throughout the Bible.

- ❖ Psalm 121:7-8(NIV) assures us, *"The LORD will keep you from all harm-- he will watch over your life; the LORD will watch over your coming and going both now and forevermore."*
- ❖ Psalm 46:1(NLT) tells us, *"God is our refuge and strength, always ready to help in times of trouble."*
- ❖ And, 2 Timothy 4:18 (NIV) reminds us, *"The Lord will rescue me from every evil attack and will bring me safely to his heavenly kingdom. To him be glory for ever and ever. Amen."*

The Bible is full of examples that show us how diligently God watches over and protects us. Daniel 6:1-24 tells us how God even protected Daniel after he was thrown into a lion's den for disobeying a law King Darius was tricked into signing.

Daniel's enemies had been looking for a way to set him up and used his love for God against him. They went to King Darius and proposed a new law that people should only pray to him. Flattered, the king approved the law, not thinking of Daniel's devotion to God.

Daniel, knowing about the law, continued to go to his window three times a day, open it and pray to God like he always had. King Darius, who actually liked Daniel, was backed into a corner and had no choice but to throw him into the lion's den, since a king could not go back on a law once it was in effect.

The story tells us that the king was extremely worried about Daniel's well being and couldn't sleep thinking about what would happen to him. However, when he went to check on Daniel the next morning, he was relieved to see Daniel was alive and not harmed by the lions at all. He didn't even have a scratch on him! King Darius helped him climb out and immediately ordered the men who tricked him into signing the law thrown into the pit.

Daniel 6:24(NIV) tells us, *"At the king's command, the men who had falsely accused Daniel were brought in and thrown into the lions' den, along with their wives and children. And before they reached the floor of the den, the lions overpowered them and crushed all their bones."*

That example may be a bit graphic but those were the times they were living in and it demonstrates God's mighty power to protect us in the face of danger.

Now, there are many people who might argue, "But, if God protects us so well, how could He let certain events happen?" or, "If He rescues us from evil, what about *this* shooting or *that* kidnapping?"

I don't have all the answers, but I can tell you this… *this is exactly how the devil wants us to think!*

He wants to push evil to the forefront of our minds so every time it makes headlines, it plants a seed in us that chips away at our faith in God's ability to protect us. This is how he begins to convince us to live in F.E.A.R. We can't allow that to happen!

There will always be people who choose to do evil. Every time someone like that makes news, we have *one* job. It's not to become afraid, question why it happened or wonder if God fell asleep on duty that day. Isaiah 41:10(NIV) tells us exactly what that job is.

It tells us, *"So do not fear, for I am with you; do not be dismayed, for I am your God. I will strengthen you and help you; I will uphold you with my righteous right hand."*

Our job is to *not* give into F.E.A.R or be intimidated by some of the craziness that goes on in the world.

We certainly can't let those things cause us to F.E.A.R living life to the fullest. We can't hand over our peace and joy for anxiety, worry or panic just because the enemy finds people weak enough to do his work. If anything, when tragedy strikes in our world, we must learn to stick it to the devil and "Dare to Believe" that much harder in God's power to protect us!

When it comes to people who are weak enough to become the devils puppets, Deuteronomy 31:6(NIV) command us, *"Be strong and courageous. Do not be afraid or terrified because of them, for the Lord your God goes with you; he will never leave you nor forsake you."* And, Proverbs 29:25 tells us that fearing people is a dangerous trap (NLT).

Some might say, "Well, what about the victims of certain tragedies? Maybe they believed the same thing."

Again, I don't have all the answers. However, I look at it like this: when it comes to the people who lost their lives in certain incidents …we can either let that loss strengthen our belief that evil will *never* win or increase our F.E.A.R that it *will*. And, to choose F.E.A.R over faith does us absolutely no good!

When we look at people like Jillian Johnson and Mayci Breaux (the two young women who died in the Louisiana theatre shooting), all the victims in the 2012 Aurora, Colorado theatre shooting, Trayvon Martin, Michael Brown, Sandra Bland, Eric Garner, Alton Sterling, Philando Castile or any victim of violence like the cowardly attack on the church goers in Charleston, South Carolina, the Boston Marathon bombing, Columbine, the Virginia Tech shooting, the attack on Pulse Nightclub, Sandy Hook, the USS Cole or 9/11 … we are presented with a choice.

We can let the lives they lost gain ground for the enemy or we can let the lives they lost be the driving force that causes us to lean even harder on God. I choose the latter. Daring to believe in God, even in the midst of evil, is like punching the devil right in the face!

Some might wonder, *"How can something like that cause you to increase your faith in God?"* The answer is …*because it has to*!

John 1:5(NLT), tells us, *"The light shines in the darkness, and the darkness can never extinguish it."* The key word in that scripture is *never*. Our job is to never stop being the light.

Remember how the whole country came together after September 11th? Regardless of race, economic status, religion or politics? Remember how immediately after the South Carolina church shooting, the main thing the survivors wanted to express to the perpetrator was forgiveness?

No evil can overcome that type of power! Think about how much better a place the world would be if everyone upheld that sense of unity, strength and faith in God on a regular basis.

Even though in today's world, it may appear that the enemy wins some battles, we must know that the complete victory belongs to God!

For every awful headline that tempts us to live in F.E.A.R, we must search further down the page for the story of the generous person who left a waitress a thousand dollar tip because she was struggling financially.

For every minute of constant news coverage of the latest tragedy, we have to spend more time looking for the stories of homeless people who were given a place to stay, children who were given meals and school supplies and complete strangers who helped one another in their time of need. Remember, earlier in the book I talked about how we have to actively *seek* God? Well, He's still there. However, in today's world we may have to look a little harder to see Him.

But, this is how we learn to keep our peace, joy and strengthen our faith in God's power to protect us.

Yes, we have to be concerned for our safety and the safety of those we love in this crazy world. However, daring to believe in God and His power to keep us safe is how we stop the devil from turning that concern into unhealthy F.E.A.R!

This reminds me of a cartoon I saw in a magazine once. There was an astronaut about to board a space shuttle and all the way down at the bottom of the platform was his little old mother looking up at him with the words *"Call me when you get there!"*

It made me laugh but demonstrates my point perfectly. We will never stop being concerned for our safety and the safety of those we love. However, the more we believe in the power of God, the easier it will be to relax, enjoy our life and live it to the fullest!

OUR HEALTH

Another one of the enemy's favorite targets, which is closely related, is the concern we have about our health and the health of those we love. I'm fairly certain that's among the top three on many people's list. While we're on a mission to strengthen our spirits, the fact remains that we reside in human bodies. At some point during our lifetime, we may face illness, challenges and sickness. While those are all physical ailments, we can't ignore the impact that our mental state has on our health, healing and recovery. This is where the enemy likes to step in and use F.E.A.R against us.

For example, how many of you have ever been surfing the Internet and came across articles titled something like, *"The Five Warning Signs of…"* or *"The Top Foods that Cause…"* (you can fill in the blank with whatever illness is in the news at the moment).

How tempted were you to click on those articles? If you did, how long did it take you to convince yourself that you might be suffering from the disease you just read about? We do it to ourselves all the time, often without realizing it.

I had a friend tell me recently it took him five minutes to read an article on diabetes…and about four hours to convince himself that he didn't have it (which he doesn't). I'm sure the devil got a kick out of that!

While it's important to be proactive about our health and pay attention to what's going on with our bodies, the "information culture" we live in makes it really easy for the devil to turn our concern into paranoia, anxiety and F.E.A.R.

We've become our own doctors, researching every little twitch and pain on Google. We're able to diagnose ourselves with sites like WebMD. The overabundance of information available at our fingertips has become just as much a hindrance as help.

I remember walking past the television one day and hearing, *"Do you have these symptoms?"* After stopping in my tracks to watch the commercial, I began to think, *"Maybe I do have those symptoms!"* Imagine how silly I felt when the commercial turned out be a warning for women with ovarian cysts! I know I'm not the only one guilty of something like this.

We live in a world where some of the medication meant to help us has to be recalled, the foods that were good for us last week could kill us this week and we have to choose between organic, grass fed or antibiotic free meat! Sometimes this can all be a bit much. The devil loves to sit back and watch us get worked up, run around in circles and question everything when it comes to our health and well-being.

While it may be kind of humorous, we have to remember that John 10:10(NIV) warns us, *"The thief comes only to steal and kill and destroy."* If we let him make us paranoid regularly about our health and well-being, then if we ever do face a battle regarding our health…we'll be too worn out to even fight!

It's important to realize when we're going through something health-wise, that our mindset is a *crucial* part of our healing and recovery. There are numerous studies that have found that a person's mental state affects his or her ability to heal from an illness. There are studies that link things like laughter to stress reduction, improved oxygen flow to the heart and brain and reduced anxiety. Many of them even quote proverbs 17:22, *"A cheerful heart is good medicine, but a broken spirit saps a person's strength"* (NLT).

We can't let the enemy trick us into using up all of our strength before a battle even begins! Think about it… how much strength will we have to put into believing God's promises of miracles, healing and recovery…if we're worn out, tired and paranoid?

How much positive energy can we devote to our recovery if we keep getting tricked into becoming afraid of everything we read about?

How much faith can we put into believing things will turn out okay…if we've already convinced ourselves that they won't?

I believe information is a wonderful thing. It can help us stay proactive when it comes to our health. However, we can get overwhelmed, distracted and forget about God's compassion, mercy and power. We can get worked up, worried and forget that He *still* performs miracles and heals people every day. This is something that, if we're faced with health issues, we *cannot* afford to forget!

I could write another whole book on how much The Bible reassures us of the healing power of God. I could fill chapters with stories of how many times Jesus healed people throughout his journey. We have to remember that Hebrews 13:8(NIV) tells us, *"Jesus Christ is the same yesterday and today and forever."* That means the same healing miracles He performed then…He still does today!

We can't let the overflow of information available at our fingertips scare us into forgetting that. We can't focus so much on the news, the Internet or even the doctor's report that we become afraid and take our eyes off The Lord. Remember what happened to Peter when he took his eyes off The Lord? He began to sink!

Matthew 9:20-22 tells the story of a woman who had been suffering from a blood disease for twelve years. Matthew 9:21 (NIV) tells us, *"She said to herself, "If I only touch his cloak, I will be healed."*

It's very important to remember what happened next. Matthew 9:22(NIV) tells us, *"Jesus turned and saw her. 'Take heart, daughter,' he said, 'your faith has healed you.' And the woman was healed at that moment."*

That woman was on a mission! She didn't get distracted. She didn't take her eyes off Jesus and knew that if she got close to Him, she would be healed. I've said it before and I'll say it again, we *all* have faith, but where we choose to place it is completely up to us! This woman's healing is a perfect example.

Instead of letting the enemy trick us into becoming paranoid and fearful by falling into the "information trap", we have to "Dare to Believe" in scriptures like:

- ❖ 1 Peter 2:24(GWT) which tells us, *"Christ carried our sins in his body on the cross so that freed from our sins, we could live a life that has God's approval. His wounds have healed you."*
- ❖ We have to believe, without a doubt, scriptures like James 5:15 (NIV) which tells us, *"And the prayer offered in faith will make the sick person well; the Lord will raise them up. If they have sinned, they will be forgiven."*
- ❖ And, we have to do what it says in Proverbs 3:7-8 (ESV) and, *"Be not wise in your own eyes; fear the Lord, and turn away from evil. It will be healing to your flesh and refreshment to your bones."*

If you happen to be going through something health –wise, I urge you to go back and re-read Section 3, "The Power of Positivity".

It's crucial that you distance yourself from negative words, thoughts, mindsets and people. It's important that you avoid falling into the enemy's traps of paranoia, panic and anxiety that are all around us. You have to be careful what you say, hear, read, do and think about, because *now*, all of that is a part of your healing process. It's vital to close any door that the enemy can use to sneak in and attack your faith.

You can't leave any room for him to attack your thoughts with doubt, hopelessness or F.E.A.R ...no matter what the situation may look like! Surround yourself with positivity and concentrate on God's promises of good health and healing. Doing so will do you a world of good!

OUR FINANCES

The last concern I want to talk about that the enemy loves to turn into F.E.A.R is, you guessed it...our finances. It seems like the cost of everything is on the rise. Everything from groceries to gas, rent, clothes and education to prescription medication and taxes have seen a hike over the last few years. The enemy knows it's a struggle for many people to stay afloat and reminds us of it every chance he gets.

It used to be that just lower and middle class families felt the pressure of the economy, but nowadays, it's a top concern for almost everyone.

Wealthy people worry about the stock market, private schools, being sued, taxes and how to keep the money they have.

The less wealthy worry about how to get to where they want to be in life while making it on what they have at the moment.

College students worry about debt. Seniors worry about the high cost of prescriptions. It goes on and on. Not having enough is a concern that seems to affect almost all of us.

The devil doesn't have to do too much to turn this concern into F.E.A.R. All he has to do is remind some of us what is (or what isn't) in our bank account, wallets and purses. It's easy to get scared when the bills that come in each month outweigh the resources we have. It's a natural reaction to become anxious, worried or even depressed when trying to figure out how to make ends meet.

It would be naïve to sit here and write about how we can't let the enemy send us into a panic over finances when I know some people have a hard time just putting food on the table. However, what I *can* do is help you shift your worry and use that energy for something more beneficial.

Instead of focusing on what we lack, I want to encourage you to "Dare to Believe" in the power of the Lord to provide! It might not be an immediate fix for whatever financial situation you're facing …but neither is giving into F.E.A.R and worrying excessively about how you'll get through it. Sometimes, we just need to remind ourselves that God is still in control.

When I was younger, my favorite aunt gave me a book called *Jesus, the Provider*. It's a picture book that tells the story of Matthew 14:13-21, where Jesus fed five thousand people with only five loaves of bread and two fish. It tells the story with illustrations and incorporates the names of my three cousins and I as a way to get kids excited about the Bible. Even though I'm a grown man, I've always kept that book on my coffee table to remind me just how much God can do once we put our trust in Him to provide.

- ❖ Luke 12:24(NIV) tells us, *"Consider the ravens: They do not sow or reap, they have no storeroom or barn; yet God feeds them. And how much more valuable you are than birds!"*
- ❖ Philippians 4:19(ESV) tells us, *"And my God will supply every need of yours according to his riches in glory in Christ Jesus."*
- ❖ And, Matthew 6:31-32(ESV) instructs us, *"Therefore do not be anxious, saying, 'What shall we eat?' or 'What shall we drink?' or 'What shall we wear?' For the Gentiles seek after all these things, and your heavenly Father knows that you need them all."*

Trusting God to meet our needs is something people had to do all throughout the Bible. Looking at some of those examples can remind us just how creative God can be when it comes to getting us what we need.

The book of Exodus tells us about the Israelites journey through the wilderness. Moses, who was instructed by God to flee Egypt and head toward the Promised Land, was leading them. It was a hard, rough journey that took a toll on them physically, mentally and tested their faith. They were tired, hungry and when they ran out of food, began to question their voyage. Exodus 16:1 tells us that, after two months of traveling, the Israelites began to turn on Moses and his brother Aaron.

"If only the LORD had killed us back in Egypt," they moaned. *"There we sat around pots filled with meat and ate all the bread we wanted. But now you have brought us into this wilderness to starve us all to death"* (Exodus 16:3, NLT).

The scripture continues, telling us in Exodus 16:12(NIV), the Lord appears to Moses and tells him, *"I have heard the grumbling of the Israelites. Tell them, 'At twilight you will eat meat, and in the morning you will be filled with bread. Then you will know that I am the LORD your God."*

That evening, a large number of quail came and covered the camp. The next morning, the ground was wet with dew. However, when the dew cleared, thin flakes almost like frost remained.

The Israelites had no idea what this substance was until Moses told them, *"It is the bread the LORD has given you to eat"* (Exodus 16:15). They called it "manna" and the Bible describes it as white and tasting like "wafers made with honey". The Israelites would even make it into cakes and bake it. Manna continued to appear for the next six days. Even though none appeared on the seventh, the double portion they were instructed to gather on the sixth day lasted on the Sabbath without spoiling.

The Bible tells us that manna rained down from Heaven in this pattern for the Israelites entire forty-year journey (yes, you read that right…*forty* years!). God even instructed Moses to gather a jar of it to save so future generations could see how the Lord provided for His people. He had his brother, Aaron, place a jar of it in the Ark of the Covenant, (a sacred chest built by the Israelites), along with the tablets of the Ten Commandments.

When they finally reached the Promised Land and were able to eat the food there, the Bible tells us the manna stopped appearing and was never seen again. If that isn't a testimony to God's power to provide…I don't know what is!

Now, does this mean we should go outside and wait for what we need to fall from the sky? No, but it does mean we should exercise that type of faith when we believe in God's ability to provide for us. We should never underestimate His ability to meet our needs!

I'm pretty sure everyone reading this can think of a few times where the Lord made a way for you when you couldn't see one. I know I certainly can!

Even though the enemy tried to use F.E.A.R to convince you each of those times would end in ruin…they didn't. Even though you may have been in the "wilderness", God provided His own version of "manna" and saw you through. We can't let F.E.A.R make us forget that!

The Bible speaks extensively about God's ability to not only provide for us…but also provide in abundance!

- ❖ Deuteronomy 28:11-12 (NIV) tells us, *"The LORD will grant you abundant prosperity--in the fruit of your womb, the young of your livestock and the crops of your ground--in the land he swore to your ancestors to give you. The LORD will open the heavens, the storehouse of his bounty, to send rain on your land in season and to bless all the work of your hands. You will lend to many nations but will borrow from none."*
- ❖ Psalms 1:1-3(ESV) assures us, *"Blessed is the man who walks not in the counsel of the wicked, nor stands in the way of sinners, nor sits in the seat of scoffers; but his delight is in the law of the LORD, and on his law he meditates day and night. He is like a tree planted by streams of water that yields its fruit in its season, and its leaf does not wither. In all that he does, he prospers."*
- ❖ And, 2 Corinthians 9:8 (NLT) promises us, *"And God will generously provide all you need. Then you will always have everything you need and plenty left over to share with others."*

Even if you don't feel like you're experiencing God's abundance at this particular moment, I want to encourage you to stay strong and not let the devil turn your concern about what you lack into F.E.A.R.

Remember, Deuteronomy 7:9 (GWT) encourages us to, *"Keep in mind that the LORD your God is [the only] God. He is a faithful God, who keeps his promise and is merciful to thousands of generations of those who love him and obey his commands."*

Also, Deuteronomy 8:18 (ESV) tells us, *"You shall remember the LORD your God, for it is he who gives you power to get wealth, that he may confirm his covenant that he swore to your fathers, as it is this day."*

It may take a shift in focus, believing in yourself enough to try a new career or stepping out on faith to start a business. Whatever the solution, God will provide everything you need to live in His abundant promises!

The subjects of our safety, health and finances are just a few of the top concerns many of us share. Even though the enemy tries to convince us otherwise, we have to know that God is still in control when it comes to these things! He is all mighty and His power does not falter!

Job 26:7-14 (NLT) assures us, *"God stretches the northern sky over empty space and hangs the earth on nothing. He wraps the rain in his thick clouds, and the clouds don't burst with the weight. He covers the face of the moon, shrouding it with his clouds. He created the horizon when he separated the waters; he set the boundary between day and night. The foundations of heaven tremble; they shudder at his rebuke. By his power the sea grew calm. By his skill he crushed the great sea monster. His Spirit made the heavens beautiful and his power pierced the gliding serpent. These are just the beginning of all that he does, merely a whisper of his power. Who, then, can comprehend the thunder of his power?"*

It doesn't matter if we're concerned about our safety in the current state of the world, our health every time we read an article on the Internet, our finances when we look in our wallet or something else completely different. There is no need to let the devil cause us to F.E.A.R any of it. God has already given us reassurance of His power over *each* and *every* one of our worries! Now, the only thing left to ask ourselves is … will we "Dare to Believe"?

CHAPTER 15

ENOY YOUR LIFE!

"I came that they may have and enjoy life, and have it in abundance to the full, till it overflows," (John 10:10, AMP).

The above scripture from John 10:10 is pretty awesome. It's a simple reminder of one of the things God desires for us to do the most. No, it's not to be perfect, criticize and judge those who aren't or to go around pointing out what everyone else is doing wrong. It's not to spend our days under the devil's boot, living in F.E.A.R or working without reward. It's simply to enjoy life.

Jesus tells us in John 10:10 that He came so we can have and enjoy life *in abundance*. However, it seems that somewhere along the way, many of us have forgotten how to do that. Whether it's due to the pressures of everyday life, the stress and responsibilities that come along with being an adult or one of the many aspects of F.E.A.R we have been talking about, enjoying life just doesn't seem to rank very high on our "to-do" list most of the time.

I thought writing about enjoying life would be a perfect way to end the section on F.E.A.R. It's something God wants desperately for us to do, the enemy tries to stop us from doing and it is actually a very powerful way to fight F.E.A.R.

In this chapter, "Enjoy Your Life", I want to take a look at a few of the things that stop us from enjoying life and how we can make an effort to correct them. I want to show you how doing so can help us learn to put more trust in God, exercise our faith, crush the enemy and help us live a happier, healthier life. Many of you may have never thought of enjoying life as away to fight back against the devil. However, by the end of this chapter, I hope you will add it to your arsenal of weapons and ways to fight back against the enemy!

Let me start by asking you this; have you ever noticed the way little kids go about their day? They play, laugh, joke, talk non- stop, are silly and don't seem to have a care in the world. While as adults, it's not practical to live every moment of our busy lives this way…we can certainly learn a thing or two from children. In fact, Jesus tells us in Matthew 18:3(NIV), *"Truly I tell you, unless you change and become like little children, you will never enter the kingdom of heaven."*

But, what does that mean? Does it mean we should go around stomping through mud puddles, jumping in piles of leaves, running through the neighborhood, spinning around in circles and climbing trees? Well, it certainly wouldn't hurt, but I would love to see the look on your neighbors face when you do!

What it means for us as adults is that we need to try our best to exhibit the same carefree, hopeful, faithful and fearless attitude that children have. Think about it; there isn't much that holds them back from enjoying life. As a matter of fact, if you come across a child who is unhappy, worried, fearful, anxious or stressed, the first thing you would think is, *"This isn't normal."*

That child would be encouraged to break out of his or her shell, be more outgoing and may even end up in therapy or on medication!

Well, if it's so unusual to see a child not enjoying his or her life… why does it become normal for us once we become adults? Sure, we've added a few bills and problems to the equation. However, even with all the added responsibilities of being an adult, we have to remember that we are still *God's* children and He wants to see us enjoy ourselves!

Still, we have been programmed to believe that a carefree way of thinking has to stop once we reach a certain age. We schedule vacations, work all year to spend a few holidays and get-togethers with our family and often put off things we would like to do for ourselves for a variety of different reasons.

Once we cross over into "adulthood", it's almost weird to see someone who is lighthearted, carefree, happy and who has a childlike faith and optimism. We may think, *"What's wrong with them?"* or *"I need whatever prescription they're on!"* When, in actuality …this is the time we need to hold on to that attitude the most!

As we go through life, many of us have experiences that cause us to become jaded, cynical, guarded, distrustful, fearful and skeptical of people and the world around us. Every day we're faced with stress and responsibilities. These things take a toll on our ability to just relax and enjoy the life Jesus died for us to have. We start to think of life as something that has to be *endured* instead of *enjoyed*. So, how do we go about reversing that mindset?

The first thing I want to talk about that stops us from fully enjoying life is …overthinking. As adults, we feel the need to have everything figured out. Sure, we all need some sort of roadmap for our life that requires us to plan ahead and think about our future. However, the sheer number of things we try to figure out on a daily basis is staggering.

From the time our feet hit the floor, we try to figure everything out from the weather, to traffic, to what to wear, what to eat and what the rest of our day will be like. And, this is before we even brush our teeth in the morning!

While there is nothing wrong with wondering about things, living everyday life this way has made us spoiled. It's put us in the habit of wanting all the answers. Now, you may be thinking, *"Well, what's wrong with that?"*

While wanting the answers to little things doesn't seem to pose any threat, it could be setting us up for a big downfall when it comes to enjoying life.

What happens when we are faced with situations where the answers aren't so obvious? What happens when we come up against something that we can't figure out as easily as the weather, the traffic or what's for dinner?

What happens when we're faced with bills we can't pay, a decision to relocate, to start a new career or different, frightening or even exciting situations we've never faced before? We tend to overthink.

Trying to figure out the answers to situations we have no obvious solution for destroys our ability to enjoy life. It often leads us down a treacherous path. It can open up the door for F.E.A.R, panic, anxiety, dread and stress. Overthinking keeps us from being able to fully enjoy life because we're too busy trying to figure it all out!

Overthinking causes us to ponder over situations, obsess over the "what-ifs", become double minded and worry. Without even realizing it, overthinking closes the door on God and throws it wide open for the devil. It gives him permission to fill our head with whatever he wants.

However, Matthew 6:25-27(NIV) gives us some great advice, *"Therefore I tell you, do not worry about your life, what you will eat or drink; or about your body, what you will wear. Is not life more important than food and the body more important than clothes? Look at the birds of the air; they do not sow or reap or store away in barns, and yet your heavenly Father feeds them. Are you not much more valuable than they? Who of you by worrying can add a single hour to his life?"*

Let me ask you this…how many of you have ever over-thought a situation and actually ended up more positive, optimistic and hopeful about it? I'm guessing not many.

When we overthink things, our thoughts are like a snowball rolling downhill. The situation starts off small in our mind and as we roll it over and over in our head, it gains momentum and starts to take on a life of it's own. It often ends up a huge, massive, negative mess that we have to try and climb out from under. Now, who can enjoy life like that?

Overthinking is one of the sneakiest ways for the devil to torment us. He uses it to confuse us, make us miserable, distract us from trusting God and to stop us from enjoying life.

1 Corinthians 14:33(ESV) tells us, *"For God is not a God of confusion but of peace."* When we feel ourselves slipping into the realm of confusion when trying to figure something out, that's a huge sign that we are overthinking. It's the first indicator that we are headed in the wrong direction and need to hand the situation over to God and relax.

It may be hard to do but Philippians 4:6(NLT) encourages us by saying, *"Don't worry about anything; instead, pray about everything. Tell God what you need, and thank him for all he has done."*

Still, when faced with situations in life where we don't have immediate answers, many of us lack the *childlike* faith to do just that. When we have exhausted all of our options, racked our brains trying to solve a problem and hit a brick wall, some of us *still* find it hard to simply pray, give the situation to God and trust Him to work it out. The enemy gets a huge kick out of that!

We don't just do it with the serious situations in life either. Many of us tend to overthink the good things in our life as well, which can suck all the fun right out of them!

I went through a really tough period in my life where I would overthink everything. I would ruin something as simple as a trip to the movies or a night out with friends with overthinking. I would want to know what time everyone was leaving, where we would meet, how many of us were driving, who was riding with who and what we were doing afterward. I would be mentally exhausted and frustrated before I even left the house!

Being a musician with no manager, every show gave me the opportunity to overthink. Since there are three people in my group, Young, Fly & Dangerous, I would want to know how many microphones were going to be set up. I had to know if they were corded or cordless, what kind of crowd was at the venue, what the sound system was like, how much time we got onstage, what we were wearing, if we had to watch our language and the list went on and on.

I would often look at my group members and think, *"Why am I the only one stressing about this?"* I would wonder why I was trying to figure everything out when many times, all they wanted to do was be able to remember their lyrics!

Well, after many nights of not having the right number of microphones, sound systems going out, the wrong version of our song being played and other mishaps, I decided to let all that go. I saw no matter how much overthinking I did, what was going to happen ...was going to happen. I could either relax and enjoy the ride or hold on with clenched teeth and white knuckles the whole time.

Performing with my group was supposed to be fun. I enjoyed doing it, but I was draining all the life out of it by thinking too much. After all, no matter what we came up against, we always managed to roll with the punches. We always had fun, gave a great show and left the crowd wanting more. We even managed to get nominated for a few awards along the way!

As simple as it may seem, experiences like those helped me learn to relax, have fun and trust God more. I saw that no matter how wrong the situation went in my eyes, God always managed to make it right. Little by little, I learned to apply that same type of trust to other areas of my life. It takes effort but it's necessary for us to build a strong faith and be able to enjoy life.

I want you to take a minute and think of any area in your life that you may be ruining with overthinking. I'm pretty sure you can come up with a few. It could be something you're doing at work, in your relationships or even something that's supposed to be fun like going on vacation or getting together with friends.

Once we understand the process, it makes it easier to catch ourselves when our thoughts begin to snowball and take on a life of their own. It makes it easier to say, "Okay, enough! I know where this is headed."

Over time, you'll learn that no matter how much energy you put into trying to figure something out...God already has it worked out *far* better than we ever could. Sometimes, we just need to relax and give Him a chance to prove it!

Trusting God more allows us to do something else that will help us enjoy life better. It makes it easier for us to cast our care.

When you really think about it, *not* knowing everything about a situation can be sort of exciting. It can add a sense of much needed adventure to our often routine lives. It helps us build our faith, lean on God and gives Him a chance to show that He's had our back all along.

Recently, a buddy of mine helped me understand how important it is to cast your care in certain situations in order to enjoy life.

Not too long ago, we decided to take a road trip. It was a long trip across several states. It was the furthest either one of us had ever driven and to a city neither one of us had visited before.

Automatically, I went into planning mode trying to figure everything out. I arranged the hotel, booked tickets for a convention we wanted to attend and started researching the best route for us to travel. I knew this particular city was notoriously bad for traffic and wanted to have all of our plans laid out before us.

However, any time I tried to discuss the trip with my buddy, he didn't have much to say. When I tried to go over the details, he didn't show any interest and didn't seem to care one way or another. I began to think, *"What's wrong with him?"* I mean, here I was, knocking myself out arranging everything and he wasn't helping or even offering any feedback.

One day, we were hanging out and I asked him, "Are you even excited about this trip?" What he said to me was one of the strangest things I had ever heard. He said, "Sure, I'm excited. But, the more details I know about the trip, the more opportunity I have to overthink them. So, instead …I'm trying not to think about them at all."

Now, I'm one of those people who likes to have a solid plan in place, so the thought that someone was okay *not* knowing the details and could just cast their care like that blew my mind.

However, what I didn't realize is that he was nervous about stepping outside his comfort zone. We were about to get on the road and venture hundreds of miles away to a city we had never been. So, every detail I gave him had the potential to send him careening down a road of "what-ifs".

The more details he had about the trip, the traffic, what route we should take, the hotel and convention …the more chances the devil had to lure him into overthinking every one of them.

He knew it would be very easy to give the enemy the opportunity to turn something fun and adventurous into something he would become anxious about and dread. So, his solution was to cast his care and not think about it at all. I'm sure you are all familiar with the phrase "ignorance is bliss". Well, he made that his motto where this trip was concerned!

He is a very responsible guy, holds a good job, pays his bills on time and stays on top of his business. However, in this case the less he thought about the situation, the more he knew he would enjoy himself.

He said, "I just want to get on the road, put the address in the GPS and go."

Once I understood this, it took the pressure off me! I thought, *"Hey, if casting his care will help him enjoy the trip better, then that's cool. Let me give it a try and see how it works."*

I prayed about it and left all the details up to God. Needless to say, we packed up the car, hit the road and had the time of our lives!

It was that road trip that made me realize it's okay to not have everything figured out. It's okay to not have every detail mapped out before us. Sure, we would like to have everything in our life laid out nicely before us, but if we don't…that's okay too. Sometimes, we just have to pack up, hit the highway and enjoy the adventures of life!

Psalm 55:22(NIV) encourages us to, *"Cast your cares on the LORD and he will sustain you; he will never let the righteous be shaken.* And, 1 Peter 5:7 (NLT) lets us know it's okay to, *"Give all your worries and cares to God, for he cares about you."*

I'm sure everyone reading this knows that one person who has casting his or her care down to a science. They never really give too much thought to anything. They sort of fly by the seat of their pants and go wherever life takes them. They're usually the friend that always has an interesting story to tell. I'm sure that despite going through their fair share of ups and downs…things always seem to work out okay for them.

I'm not saying we should forgo planning, do away with being prepared, thinking ahead and go whatever way the wind blows us. However, we may need to take a page from their book once in a while and trade in our same old routine for a brand new adventure. We may even end up with a few interesting stories of our own to tell!

When we put our trust in God, cast our care and step out on faith …we will see that He's *always* along for the ride!

That trip also taught me another important aspect for enjoying life … living in the moment. As we get older, we tend to always consider the impact our actions will have on other parts of our life.

We tend to think things like, *"I can't stay out too late because I have to get up in the morning."* Or, *"There's no way I can take a vacation right now because I have too many things on my plate."*

There's nothing wrong with that sort of thinking. After all, it's an important part of being a responsible person. However, many people live their entire lives this way. Some of you have a "bucket list" so long, even if you put this book down and started on it right now …you wouldn't have enough time left in life to accomplish even half of it. Why is that?

Again, once we become adults, enjoying life has a tendency to get pushed further down our priority list. Many people give up their dreams, hobbies, goals and things they've always wanted to do because they don't know how to live in the moment and go for it.

When it comes to enjoying life, I get inspiration from scriptures like 1Corinthians 9:24(NIV), which asks us, *"Do you not know that in a race all the runners run, but only one gets the prize? Run in such a way as to get the prize."*

However, we've traded in our *"win"* mindset for a *"when"* mindset. "I'll enjoy life *when…*" or "I'll pursue my goals *when…*" It's that mindset that holds us back from so many great things in life.

I want everyone reading this who is of a certain age to stop and think back to when you were a teenager. I bet there was nothing that stopped you from doing what you wanted to do, when you wanted to do it. You probably didn't think about any sort of repercussions at all.

Now, I'm sure that kind of thinking might have gotten you in some trouble a time or two. However, I also bet you look back on those days as some of the best times of your life. I know I do!

Well, what would happen if we took just a little bit of that determination and "live in the moment" attitude and coupled it with the wisdom we've gained over the years? It would probably be a perfect recipe for the adventurous, enjoyable and balanced life we need to help us get some of our "win" back!

Nevertheless, there always seems to be something that holds us back from living in the moment and enjoying life *right now.*

- We are hindered by the present (*"I'm too busy"*).

- We are deterred by future, ("*I have next months bills to think about*")
- We are even discouraged by the past ("*I tried stepping out of my comfort zone before and it didn't work*").

Before you know it, what we thought about doing *today* becomes just another thing added to the list of things we would like to do… *some day*.

James 4:13-15(NIV) warns us, *"Now listen, you who say, 'Today or tomorrow we will go to this or that city, spend a year there, carry on business and make money.' Why, you do not even know what will happen tomorrow. What is your life? You are a mist that appears for a little while and then vanishes. Instead, you ought to say, 'If it is the Lord's will, we will live and do this or that.'"*

The scripture from John that begins this chapter (10:10, AMP) lets us know that it is *absolutely* the Lords will for us to enjoy life and have it in abundance! Yet, the following three things directly prevent us from doing so.

DISCOURAGED BY THE PAST

I know plenty of people who will not step out of the box, try new things, go new places or even order different items off a menu because of past experiences. Some people are afraid to take a chance on relationships, love, a new career, a move or any new thing they might enjoy because of past disappointments, failures and hurt.

Isaiah 43:18-19(NIV) tells us, *"Forget the former things; do not dwell on the past. See, I am doing a new thing! Now it springs up; do you not perceive it? I am making a way in the wilderness and streams in the wasteland."*

It's sad to think that some people may never experience what God has planned for them because they're living in the past and not in the moment.

Making an effort to step out and enjoy life exposes us to new experiences, ideas, places and people. It can inspire us, motivate us and even lead us toward our destiny. We never know what God has waiting for us. However, I can tell you that it will most likely never happen as long as we live in the past, and never explore options other than what we already know.

HINDERED BY THE PRESENT

Just as harmful as living in the past is focusing too much on the present. Many people are unable to enjoy life because they can't see past some of the things hindering them at the moment. They always have an excuse as to what's holding them back or why they can't let loose, relax and enjoy life *right now*.

Psalm 118:24 (ESV) tells us, *"This is the day that the LORD has made; let us rejoice and be glad in it."* However, I know many people, (including myself) who are guilty of putting off their happiness and enjoyment until a later date because of something presently going on in their life.

For example, the whole time while working on this book I had to keep reminding myself to enjoy life. I had a very hard time relaxing, letting loose and having fun because of the huge task I was embarking on.

My family had to keep reminding me to take time for myself and enjoy some of the things I wanted to do. Even still, I felt guilty taking a day to go to the movies, hang out with friends or even reading a book that wasn't related to work in some way. I found myself stressed, miserable and in desperate need of some fun.

I know there are many people that find themselves in the same predicament. When you think about the number of people living life like this every day, is it any wonder why our stress levels are higher than ever before, our blood pressure is through the roof and the enemy is able to set us off at the drop of a dime?

Still, none of that will change unless we make an effort to do some things differently. For example, how many times have you woken up, seen it was a nice day outside, thought of something you would like to do…and never did it.

Many people use work as an excuse. Yet, those are some of the same people who find themselves in a mad rush at the end of the year to use vacation days they have accumulated in order not to lose them. My question is ... "Why wait?"

There will always be something going on in our lives that can hold us back from enjoying the moment...if we let it. We all have jobs, families and responsibilities but if we wait until the time is "right" to enjoy life...we could be waiting forever!

It won't hurt us to take some time for ourselves more often ...despite what we have going on at the moment.

As a matter of fact, I would like to challenge you all to do something. The next time you pick up this book to read it, make it a point to do something enjoyable just for yourself. Sit down at Starbucks and order one of those fancy, overpriced drinks or take it to the beach and enjoy the sun and sand. Go to a park or sit by a pool. If it's cold and raining, relax in your bed or on the couch in your pajamas. Just make a special effort to live in the moment and do whatever you want to do to enjoy yourself...despite all that you may have going on. Remember, it's Gods *will* for us to do so!

DETERRED BY THE FUTURE

The last thing that stops us from living in the moment and enjoying life is something I could write another whole book on...worrying about the future. I'm sure even as you're reading this, there are a number of things running through your mind for later today, tomorrow, a week from now, next month or even next year.

When it comes to worrying about the future, Matthew 6:34(NLT) tells us, *"So don't worry about tomorrow, for tomorrow will bring its own worries. Today's trouble is enough for today."*

I find it very interesting that *every* version of James 4:14 makes it a point to tell us how short our life is.

- One version refers to us as a *"mist that appears for a little while and then vanishes,"* (NIV).

- Another says our life, *"is like the morning fog...it's here a little while, then it's gone,"*(NLT).
- Yet, another tells us, *"You are just a vapor that appears for a little while and then vanishes away,"* (NASB).

I mean really, how many ways does the Bible have to tell us that life is short?

Don't let living in the moment and enjoying life escape you because your mind is occupied with things that haven't even happened yet!

When it comes to living in the moment, I remember an experience that really drove home the idea.

One year I went on a trip to Jamaica. It was something I had always wanted to do. As soon as I checked in and went to my room, I immediately noticed something ...there was no clock in the room. Thinking that this was a mistake I called the front desk.

In her West Indian accent, the receptionist told me, "Oh no, it's no mistake. We want you to enjoy yourself and live in the moment. So, relax and don't worry about anything, not even the time!"

Well, I took her advice and had one of the most enjoyable, stress free times of my life!

While it's not a practical way to live all the time, that advice on living in the moment is something I always try to remember when I need a reminder to enjoy life a little more. And, I want you all to remember it as well!

1 Chronicles 29:15 tells us, *"We are here for only a moment, visitors and strangers in the land as our ancestors were before us. Our days on earth are like a passing shadow, gone so soon without a trace."*

When you think about it like that, it really puts it in perspective, doesn't it? All the things that stop us from enjoying life don't seem so big anymore, do they? Remember, we're here to enjoy every moment Jesus died for us to have.

So, what's holding you back? Stop overthinking, learn to cast your care, "Enjoy Your Life", live in the moment and give God a chance to show you He's there ...every step of the way!

SECTION 6

THIS IS THE REMIX!

CHAPTER 16

JESUS, THE REBEL

"Therefore, since we are surrounded by such a great cloud of witnesses, let us throw off everything that hinders and the sin that so easily entangles. And let us run with perseverance the race marked out for us, fixing our eyes on Jesus, the pioneer and perfecter of faith. For the joy set before him he endured the cross, scorning its shame, and sat down at the right hand of the throne of God" (Hebrews 12:1-2, NIV).

What comes to mind when you think of Jesus? I'm sure it could be any number of amazing things: *Healer, Protector, Savior, Provider, Son of God, Warrior… Friend.* While all of these things are absolutely true, have you ever taken the time to think about the actual person behind that awesome name?

Have you ever sat down and really thought about the type of person Jesus had to be in order to see His destiny through to the end and make such an everlasting impact along the way?

Sure, we know Him as a Teacher, Prophet, Messiah, King, Redeemer, Counselor, Deliverer, High Priest and Lord of All. But, have you ever wondered what it took for Him to *be* all those things?

The Bible tells us many wonderful things about Jesus. It lets us know that He is:

- ❖ *Loving,* (John 3:16, Revelations 1:5)
- ❖ *Compassionate,* (Luke 7:13, Matthew 9:36)
- ❖ *Humble,* (John 13:12, 2 Corinthians 8:9)

- *Merciful,* (Mathew 15:32, Matthew 20:30-34)
- *Meek* and *Gentle,* (2 Corinthians 10:1).

Certainly, anyone who has Jesus in their life can attest to all that. I've talked about many of those things right here in this book.

However, there was also another side of Jesus. It was the side that made Him the center of attention everywhere He went. It was provocative, controversial and radical. It attracted crowds and loyal disciples who left their lives behind to follow Him. It made some people look at Him as their Savior while others see Him as their biggest threat.

It was a side that caused Him to speak His mind and stand up for what He believed in. And, it turned the world and it's religious leaders upside down. It made Him a target and would change the way people view God, religion and salvation…forever. And, it still influences over two billion people…2,000 years later. I like to call that other side "Jesus, the Rebel" and it's one of the things I find most cool about Him.

In this chapter, "Jesus, the Rebel" we'll take a look at some of the things that made Jesus a revolutionary. We'll look at some of the ways He didn't fit the mold of what some people thought the "Son of God" should be. We'll look at some of His most controversial acts, ideas and philosophies and how they ruffled more than a few religious feathers. And, we'll look at how, despite what those people thought of Him, He remained true to Himself, God and those who believed in Him.

It's my hope that by doing so, those of you reading this will find the courage to stay true to yourselves and represent Jesus in the way that's right for *you*…despite how others think that should be done. We are each a unique representation of God's love and we shouldn't let anyone put limits on how that's expressed to the world. Jesus certainly didn't!

I chose the above scripture from Hebrews because it describes Jesus as the *"pioneer"* (innovator, forerunner and creator) of faith. It also tells us that He *"scorned"* (rejected and refused) the shame of the cross.

Even though the efforts of several groups of people (the Romans and religious leaders of Israel) intended Jesus's death on the cross to cause Him shame, He rejected even their most desperate attempt to disgrace Him. He didn't let the crucifixion stop Him from proving His power and even prayed for His persecutors while on the cross by saying, *"Father, forgive them, for they do not know what they are doing"* (Luke 23:24, NIV). That act alone speaks volumes about the type of boldness Jesus possessed, even in His darkest hour.

It was that boldness and passion that were trademarks of His short life. Not much is known about the early life of Jesus. Luke 1:26-38 tells us that God sent an angel named Gabriel to a town called Nazareth in Galilee. There, he spoke to a woman named Mary, who was about to be married to a man named Joseph.

Gabriel tells her in Luke 1:31-33(NIV), *"You will conceive and give birth to a son, and you are to call him Jesus. He will be great and will be called the Son of the Most High. The Lord God will give him the throne of his father David, and he will reign over Jacob's descendants forever; his kingdom will never end."*

Confused, because she was a virgin, Mary asked the angel how this would come to be.

Luke 1:35-38(NIV) tells us, *"The angel answered, 'The Holy Spirit will come on you, and the power of the Most High will overshadow you. So the holy one to be born will be called the Son of God. Even Elizabeth your relative is going to have a child in her old age, and she who was said to be unable to conceive is in her sixth month. For no word from God will ever fail.'*

'I am the Lord's servant,' Mary answered. 'May your word to me be fulfilled.' Then the angel left her."

I guess you could say Jesus was different from the very beginning, even with the way He was conceived!

Anyone who has ever seen a Christmas manger scene knows that Mary and Joseph went on to travel to Bethlehem, where Jesus was born. I think it's interesting to mention that the prophet Mica, (who lived about seven hundred years before Jesus), declared that Bethlehem would be the birthplace of the Messiah.

In Mica 5:2 (NLT), he says, *"But you, O Bethlehem Ephrathah, are only a small village among all the people of Judah. Yet a ruler of Israel will come from you, one whose origins are from the distant past."*

At the time of Jesus's birth, (around 4BC to 8BC), a star appeared over Bethlehem. The star attracted many visitors who believed it signified the birth of a new king. Many of those visitors were familiar with the early prophecies that a Messiah would be born in Israel who would have an impact on the entire world.

The problem, however, was that Israel already had a ruler...King Herod the Great. Herod, (who wasn't even a real king), was known as a vicious man who ordered the death of many of his own family members. So, the idea that people were coming from far and wide to worship a new king didn't sit well with him at all. Herod ordered the death of every infant in Bethlehem in hopes of eliminating the newborn king.

Once again, an angel showed up and saved the day. Matthew 2:13(NLT) tells us, *"After the wise men were gone, an angel of the Lord appeared to Joseph in a dream. 'Get up! Flee to Egypt with the child and his mother,' the angel said. 'Stay there until I tell you to return, because Herod is going to search for the child to kill him."*

Mary and Joseph followed the angel's warning and took Jesus to Egypt, where they lived until King Herod died. It is unknown how long they remained there.

When it was safe, Matthew 2:19-20 tells us that, again, an angel appeared to Joseph in a dream. This time, the angel told him it was safe to take Jesus and Mary back to Israel because those who were trying to kill Him were dead.

The scripture explains that instead of going back to Judea, because Herod's son was now ruling in his place, they decided to settle in Nazareth (Matthew 2:22-23). This is where Jesus would grow up and become an adult.

Not much is known of the time between Jesus's adolescence and the beginning of His ministry at the age of thirty. However, there are a few scriptures that give us clues about His growing boldness and passion to serve God.

One instance, (Luke 2:41-52) tells us how, at the age of twelve, Jesus traveled to Jerusalem for the annual Passover Festival with His family. The scriptures tell us that after the festival was over, His parents began the journey back home. However, Jesus decided to stay behind. Because they were traveling in such a large group, it took Mary and Joseph an entire *day* to realize that Jesus wasn't with them!

After searching among their relatives and friends, with no luck, Mary and Joseph decided to head back to Jerusalem in search of Jesus.

Luke 2:46-49(NIV) reads, *"After three days they found him in the temple courts, sitting among the teachers, listening to them and asking them questions. Everyone who heard him was amazed at his understanding and his answers. When his parents saw him, they were astonished. His mother said to him, 'Son, why have you treated us like this? Your father and I have been anxiously searching for you.'*

'Why were you searching for me?' he asked. 'Didn't you know I had to be in my Father's house?'"

Now, I'm not a parent but I can only imagine what my response would have been! Can you imagine frantically searching for your child for *three days* only to find him cool as a cucumber looking at you like *you* were the crazy one? I'm sure Mary and Joseph were overjoyed, angry and even a little proud at the same time!

But, that was the type of boldness Jesus had even as a child when it came to serving God. That confidence in His mission and message was part of the reason some religious conservatives and political dictators viewed Him as a threat later on in His life.

Around the age of thirty, Jesus left Nazareth to travel to the river Jordan. There, His predecessor, John the Baptist, was drawing crowds preaching and baptizing people. John the Baptist had such an awesome following that some thought *he* was the Messiah. However, the Bible tells us that in Matthew 3:11(NLT), John the Baptist declares, *"I baptize with water those who repent of their sins and turn to God. But someone is coming soon who is greater than I am--so much greater that I'm not worthy even to be his slave and carry his sandals. He will baptize you with the Holy Spirit and with fire."*

When Jesus showed up at the river, John didn't immediately know that He was the Messiah. Still, he knew there was something different about Jesus.

Many of the people seeking baptism were hypocrites and John called them out and refused to baptize them. Yet, when Jesus showed up wanting to be baptized, Matthew 3:14-15(NLT) tells us, *"But John tried to talk him out of it. 'I am the one who needs to be baptized by you,' he said, 'so why are you coming to me?' But Jesus said, 'It should be done, for we must carry out all that God requires.' So John agreed to baptize him."*

The scripture goes on to tell us that when Jesus came up from the water, immediately heaven opened up and the spirit of God descended like a dove and settled on Him. Then, a voice rang out from heaven and said, *"This is my beloved son, with who I am well pleased"* (Matthew 3:17).

Jesus being baptized and receiving the spirit of God signifies the best thing to ever happen to us. However, it also represents the *worst* thing to ever happen to certain groups of people as well.

In John 14:6, Jesus tells his disciple Thomas, *"I am the way and the truth and the life. No one comes to the Father except through me."*

Many of you might be familiar with the movie *A Few Good Men*, where Jack Nicholson yells at Tom Cruise, *"You can't handle the truth!"* Well, that's exactly what happened.

Many hypocritical, phony, religious people who were in power couldn't handle the truth of Jesus being the Messiah. When He began preaching and gaining followers they viewed Him as a huge threat to their political and religious establishment.

Imagine how furious it must have made the Sadducees and the Pharisees, (the two main groups who ruled Israel at the time) to be opposed by someone like Jesus.

The Sadducees, (pronounced "SAD-dzhoo-seez") were wealthy aristocrats who held powerful positions in upper-class society. Jesus was the complete opposite. Since their main concern was keeping peace with the Romans, (because Israel was under Roman control at the time) they were more concerned with politics than religion.

They were very self-sufficient and often denied God's involvement in day-to-day life. They didn't believe in resurrection, the afterlife or the spiritual world (angels and demons). Jesus pretty much flew under their radar until it got to the point they were afraid He would bring unwanted attention from the Romans. That's when they plotted with their rivals, the Pharisees, to put Jesus to death.

However, it was with the Pharisees, (middle –class business men who were more in touch with the common people) that Jesus was often in direct conflict with. The Pharisees went strictly by the Old Testament. And, while they expected others to live by God's laws, they rarely followed those laws themselves.

They added their own traditions (Mark 7:7-9) and pretended to be holier than they really were.

Most of them were hypocrites who were more concerned with religion than God, gaining attention and approval from others, were unwilling to listen to Jesus and were concerned with following many unimportant rules.

I'm sure everyone reading this knows a few "religious" people who fall into that category!

It was at the point where trying to obey all the laws under the Pharisees had become an oppressive, overwhelming and unrealistic burden people struggled to live up to (Luke 11:46). Sadly, it's still like that for many people today.

This was the atmosphere of things when Jesus began His ministry, so conflict with the Pharisees was inevitable.

From the time He returned to Nazareth (after going around making somewhat of a name for Himself [Luke 4:14-15]), Jesus made it clear when He read from the scroll of Isaiah, *"The Spirit of the LORD is upon me, for he has anointed me to bring Good News to the poor. He has sent me to proclaim that captives will be released, that the blind will see, that the oppressed will be set free, and that the time of the LORD's favor has come"* (Luke 4:18-19, NLT), that He had an entirely different message when it came to salvation.

Luke 4:20 – 22 goes on to read, *"He rolled up the scroll, handed it back to the attendant, and sat down. All eyes in the synagogue looked at him intently. Then he began to speak to them. 'The Scripture you've just heard has been fulfilled this very day!' Everyone spoke well of him and was amazed by the gracious words that came from his lips. 'How can this be?' they asked. 'Isn't this Joseph's son?"*

I get a huge kick out of that scripture! I can just imagine Jesus standing there reading from the scroll, making this huge declaration that *He* is the one that is going to bring about the time of the Lord's favor, rolling the scroll back up, handing it to the attendant …and simply sitting down.

I almost laugh picturing the stunned look on people's faces as He sat there calm, cool and collected after dropping a bomb like that. Today, we would call that, saying what you have to say and "dropping the mic". Really …what could be said after that?

Jesus proclaiming to be the Messiah was a major problem for the Pharisees. To them, it meant that His Heavenly authority outweighed their own. This might not have been a problem…if Jesus had been the type of Messiah they were looking for.

Remember, the Pharisees were all about following rules to get into Heaven, gaining attention from people for doing so and how important they looked to others. Having an actual relationship with God took a backseat to religion and upholding the Law. They thought the Messiah was going to be someone of great political power, who supported that philosophy and agreed with their way of doing things. They were in no way expecting someone like Jesus… the Rebel to oppose them at every turn!

His claims probably wouldn't have meant much to them…except the crowds Jesus preached to started to believe Him as well. People can say anything they want, but when others start to listen, *that's* when it becomes a problem.

And, the crowds Jesus preached to desperately needed to hear the Good News He was bringing.

The Pharisees were the keepers of the Mosaic Law (the Law God gave to Moses in the Old Testament). The Ten Commandments were part of the Mosaic Law, however there were over *six hundred* more commandments given to the people in the Old Testament. (Go ahead, look it up!)

As if following those commandments weren't a big enough task, the Jewish leaders added their own rules, regulations and traditions over time. Many of them were difficult to live by. Some of them were so extreme that the meaning behind the law was lost altogether.

They believed the only way to gain favor with God was to uphold these Laws to the letter. They believed the ability to do so outweighed the condition of a person's heart.

So, for the people, (who you could say were "captives" of the Law) to hear about God's grace, acceptance, forgiveness, salvation, reconciliation, favor and love was something completely liberating. Being told that the Kingdom of God on Earth is something you are able to *receive* and don't have to try and *obtain* was an entirely different philosophy. Everywhere Jesus went crowds gathered and became excited when He preached.

While Jesus upheld the Law, He also brought grace into the picture. As matter of fact, He was a perfect mix of the two. John 1:17(NIV) tells us, *"For the law was given through Moses; grace and truth came through Jesus Christ."*

Still, the Pharisees weren't having it. They became angry that the crowds believed Jesus, blamed it on ignorance (John 7:48-49), constantly watched Him, tried to have Him arrested (John 7:30-32) and even tried to stone Him…a *few* times!

Even with all the great things He did, amazing miracles He performed and good news that He preached… why were they still so outraged at the idea of Jesus being the Messiah? There were several different reasons. Let's take a look.

To the Pharisees, Jesus represented a huge threat to their religious system and authority. Jesus wasn't afraid to speak His mind and certainly wasn't afraid to voice His opinion about their hypocrisy. He did so time and time again.

A clear example of what Jesus thought about the Pharisees can be seen in Matthew 23:2-6(NLT), where He tells a crowd of listeners and His disciples, *"The teachers of religious law and the Pharisees are the official interpreters of the law of Moses. So practice and obey whatever they tell you, but don't follow their example. For they don't practice what they teach. They crush people with unbearable religious demands and never lift a finger to ease the burden. Everything they do is for show. On their arms they wear extra wide prayer boxes with Scripture verses inside, and they wear robes with extra long tassels. And they love to sit at the head table at banquets and in the seats of honor in the synagogues."* ...And, that was just the *nice* part!

Never one to mince words, Jesus goes on in Matthew 23:13-39 (NLT) and continues to give His opinion of the Pharisees. Some highlights are:

- Jesus saying that they shut the door of the kingdom of Heaven in people's faces (Matthew 23:13)
- Jesus saying that the Pharisees would cross land and sea to gain one follower…then turn that person into twice the child of hell that they are (Matthew 23:15)
- Calling them blind guides (Matthew 23: 16)
- Saying even though they are careful to tithe, they ignore the more important aspects of the Law like justice, mercy and faith (Matthew 23:23)

Cleanliness was very important to the Pharisees and they associated anything unclean with sin. Jesus even says (in Matthew 23:25) that while they are carful to clean the outside of a cup and dish, inside they are filthy …full of greed and self- indulgence. He even compared them to whitewashed tombs; beautiful on the outside but on the inside full of dead peoples bones (Matthew 23:27).

That's just *one* instance where Jesus spoke of the Pharisees! I encourage you to check out Matthew 23:2-39, it's a very interesting read!

Jesus made it no secret how hypocritical the Pharisees were. To a group of people who were extremely concerned with how they looked to others…this was a huge problem.

Jesus's criticism of the religious leaders wasn't just limited to His sermons. He actually practiced what He preached and made moves to correct their wrongdoings.

One such instance takes place in John 2:13-17. The scripture tells us it was almost time for the Passover celebration, so Jesus headed to Jerusalem. When He got to the Temple area, He saw merchants selling various things like cattle, sheep and doves. Dealers had also set up tables to exchange foreign currency. Needless to say, Jesus wasn't pleased with the business dealings going on in the temple.

The Bible tells us He made a whip from some rope and chased them all out of the Temple. He drove the animals out, scattered the moneychangers coins all over the floor and even flipped over their tables! Then, He went over to the people who were selling doves and told them, *"Stop turning my Fathers house into a marketplace!"* (John 2:16, NLT)

It may seem like a scene from a reality show, but that's the type of passion Jesus had to rid the church of phony religion and hypocrisy.

Actually, the Bible tells of two accounts where Jesus "cleansed" the Temple this way. The first, I described above from John (2:13-16), which took place shortly after He began His ministry and a second time (Matthew 21:12-17), which took place shortly before He was crucified.

It wasn't just His opinion of them and boldness to do something about it that the religious leaders disapproved of. They even had a problem with the *miracles* Jesus performed. The Bible tells us of many amazing things Jesus did like:

- ❖ Healing people, (Matthew 8:14-17, Luke 5:18-26)
- ❖ Cleansing evil spirits, (Matthew 8:28-34)
- ❖ Feeding crowds of people with hardly any food at all, (Matthew 14:14-21)
- ❖ Commanding the elements, (Mark 4:37-41)
- ❖ Walking on water, (John 6:16-21)
- ❖ Even raising the dead, (Luke 8:40-56).

There are at least thirty-seven recorded miracles performed by Jesus in the gospels. However, the disciple John tells us in John 21:25(NIV), *"Jesus did many other things as well. If every one of them were written down, I suppose that even the whole world would not have room for the books that would be written."*

The Bible tells us that multitudes of people came from Israel and nations all around and gives us many examples of how Jesus healed them all. So, why in the world would the religious leaders take issue with Jesus going around doing good, healing people and performing other amazing miracles?

One issue the Pharisees had with the miracles Jesus performed (specifically healing) was that He was doing them on the Sabbath, (the seventh day set aside for rest and worship). Many people think of the Sabbath as Sunday, but it's actually *Saturday*.

Some historians say the change from Saturday to Sunday was due to:

- Growing anti- Jewish sentiment
- The Roman emperor Constantine's conversion to Christianity
- Constantine's decision to let his army of once-pagan soldiers continue to worship on the original day set aside to observe their former "Sun God" after their conversion to Christianity, (hence, the name "Sunday").

In any event, there was supposed to be no work done on the Sabbath. To break this rule, to the Pharisees, was unthinkable.

They created many different categories of what "work" meant and even more sub-categories to clarify even further. There were rules as to how many steps you could take and even how much weight you could carry on the Sabbath. There were so many rules as to what you *couldn't* do on the Sabbath that the very day set aside for rest and worship became a chore for people to adhere to!

Even today, there are many different rules for Jewish people to follow in order to observe the Sabbath. Some of them involve not driving, cooking, using the telephone, electricity, paper towels, not handling money, writing or even watering plants. After doing some research, I have to say they have come up with some very clever and innovative ways to make their lives easier while still observing the Sabbath. It's also important to note that if it comes down to saving a human life, they are allowed to do things like drive someone to the hospital in an emergency or use the telephone to call for help, even on the Sabbath.

However, in Jesus's time, the Pharisees weren't so understanding of His desire to save lives.

There were several instances where they accused Jesus of breaking the Sabbath because He healed someone. One such instance takes place in Luke 6:6-11.

Jesus was already under close watch after being accused of breaking the Sabbath because His disciples plucked off and ate heads of grain while walking through a field (Luke 6:1-5). So, the Pharisees were keeping a very close eye on Him.

Luke 6:6-11(NLT) begins telling us, *" On another Sabbath day, a man with a deformed right hand was in the synagogue while Jesus was teaching. The teachers of religious law and the Pharisees watched Jesus closely. If he healed the man's hand, they planned to accuse him of working on the Sabbath."*

However, Jesus knew what they were thinking. Being the rebel that He was and determined to do what was right, the scripture tells us He called the man up to the front of the church and said to His critics, *"I have a question for you. Does the law permit good deeds on the Sabbath, or is it a day for doing evil? Is this a day to save life or to destroy it?"* (Luke 6:9)

With that, the scripture tells us that Jesus looked at the religious leaders one by one, told the man to hold out his hand…and healed him! (Luke 6:10) Needless to say, this made His enemies furious and *"wild with rage",* (Luke 6:11, NLT).

They were so appalled that someone who claimed to be the Messiah would break the Sabbath, (even if it was to heal someone) they even claimed His power was from Satan!

After hearing how Jesus healed a demon-possessed man (Matthew 12:22), the Pharisees said, *"No wonder he can cast out demons. He gets his power from Satan, the prince of demons"* (Matthew 12:24, NLT).

Even though they were especially enraged by His disregard for not "working" on the Sabbath and healing people, it was His disregard for *many* of their "religious" rules that continued to anger the Pharisees.

Jesus knew that many of the Pharisees rules were man-made. He saw that they placed more importance on following these rules and traditions than they actually did on God. In doing so, they often missed the point of the Law altogether.

For example, the Pharisees placed extreme importance on cleanliness. However, it wasn't for the same reasons we do today. We practice good hygiene to keep up our appearance, smell good, stay clean and avoid germs. We may wash our hands or use hand sanitizer after coming in contact with a dirty gas pump, shopping cart handle, ATM machine or before we eat. We clean and handle our food a certain way to avoid getting sick. And, we take care of ourselves and our surroundings to maintain a healthy lifestyle.

However, the Pharisees washed in order to cleanse themselves of much more than germs. They associated anything unclean with *sin*. They would wash in order to cleanse themselves of any defilement or sin they may have picked up from associating with items, animals or even people.

If they were in the marketplace, they would ritually cleanse themselves when they came home. They wouldn't do it because the marketplace or meat was dirty, but because they may have come in contact with something or someone they considered to be "unclean" such as a Gentile (someone who isn't Jewish).

They believed certain foods and animals were either clean or unclean. If a "clean" animal was slaughtered improperly…it became "unclean". If something were "unclean", then contact with that item made a person "unclean". Even today, Jewish people have very strict guidelines about what's okay and not okay to eat and many rules on how things have to be prepared. This is what it means to have a "kosher" diet.

In Jesus's time, cleanliness was so important to the keepers of the Law because they believed defilement and sin came from *outside* sources. So, much so, that they ignored the importance of inside factors like the mind, heart and spirit. Their idea of holiness revolved around identifying what could make them "unclean" and avoiding contact with it at all cost.

There are several times in the Bible where the Pharisees took issue with Jesus or the disciples because they ate without washing their hands. Again, this wasn't the type of scolding you would give a child who sat down to eat after playing outside. This represented much more to the Pharisees.

Mark 7:1-8 tells us how the Pharisees and other teachers of the Law came to Jesus after seeing some of the disciples eating without cleansing their hands and asked Him, *"Why don't your disciples live according to the tradition of the elders instead of eating their food with defiled hands?"* (Mark 7:5, NIV)

Oh boy…what did they do that for? This prompted Jesus…the Rebel to put them in their place, yet again!

Mark 7:6-9 (NIV) tells us, *"He replied, 'Isaiah was right when he prophesied about you hypocrites; as it is written: These people honor me with their lips, but their hearts are far from me. They worship me in vain; their teachings are merely human rules.'*

You have let go of the commands of God and are holding on to human traditions. And he continued, 'You have a fine way of setting aside the commands of God in order to observe your own traditions!"

After telling the Pharisees off and giving them a quick lesson about honoring their mother and father (Mark 7:10-13), Jesus called the crowd to Him and said, *"Listen to me, everyone, and understand this. Nothing outside a person can defile them by going into them. Rather, it is what comes out of a person that defiles them."* (Mark 7:14-15, NIV)

Jesus even got a little irritated with the disciples after they asked Him what all that meant.

Mark 7:18-23(NIV) tells us how Jesus responded, *"Are you so dull?" He asked. 'Don't you see that nothing that enters a person from the outside can defile them? For it doesn't go into their heart but into their stomach, and then out of the body.'(In saying this, Jesus declared all foods clean.) He went on: 'what comes out of a person is what defiles them. For it is from within, out of a person's heart, that evil thoughts come--sexual immorality, theft, murder, adultery, greed, malice, deceit, lewdness, envy, slander, arrogance and folly. All these evils come from inside and defile a person."*

Again, the religious leaders couldn't handle the truth and certainly couldn't handle it coming from someone like Jesus!

If they had such a huge issue with Him and the disciples being "unclean" with sin because they didn't do something as simple as wash their hands before eating, imagine how much more of an issue they had with something else they thought made Jesus unworthy of being the Messiah…the company He kept.

The Pharisees were very arrogant and prided themselves on not associating with sinners. Even if they accidentally came into contact with someone who they believed to be a sinner, they thought their ritual cleansing would keep the sin at bay. While they boasted of the fact they didn't keep the company of sinners …Jesus did the opposite and welcomed them.

One instance tells us about Jesus having dinner with Matthew at his home. Matthew 9:10(NIV) explains, *"While Jesus was having dinner at Matthew's house, many tax collectors and sinners came and ate with him and his disciples."*

Of course, the Pharisees were keeping a close watch on Jesus, so they saw this. They went to the disciples (I guess by then they knew better than to go to Jesus directly!) and asked them why their teacher ate with sinners.

Matthew 9:12-13 tells us, *"On hearing this, Jesus said, 'It is not the healthy who need a doctor, but the sick. But go and learn what this means: 'I desire mercy, not sacrifice.' For I have not come to call the righteous, but sinners."*

Luke 36:50 tells us of another instance where Jesus stood up for sinners. The scripture tells us that one of the Pharisees invited Him over for dinner. There were actually a few of them who were willing to listen to what Jesus had to say and get close to Him to try and figure Him out.

A woman with a "sinful" past (I'll leave that to your imagination) knew Jesus was there and came over. She had a small alabaster jar of perfume with her that she probably wanted to use to anoint Jesus's forehead as a sign of respect.

However, when she saw Jesus, she became overwrought with emotion and started to cry. The scripture tells us that she cried so hard that she began to wet His feet with her tears. Then, she knelt down and wiped His feet with her hair, kissed them over and over and anointed them with the perfume.

Luke 7:39(NIV) tells us, *"When the Pharisee who had invited him saw this, he said to himself, "If this man were a prophet, he would know who is touching him and what kind of woman she is--that she is a sinner."*

The scripture goes on to say that Jesus tells the Pharisee a story of a man who lent two people money. One person was lent a greater amount than the other. The man decided to forgive both debts and then Jesus asked him, *"Which do you think was more grateful?"*

Luke 7:43-47 says, *"Simon replied, 'I suppose the one who had the bigger debt forgiven.' 'You have judged correctly,' Jesus said. Then he turned toward the woman and said to Simon, 'Do you see this woman? I came into your house. You did not give me any water for my feet, but she wet my feet with her tears and wiped them with her hair. You did not give me a kiss, but this woman, from the time I entered, has not stopped kissing my feet. You did not put oil on my head, but she has poured perfume on my feet. Therefore, I tell you, her many sins have been forgiven--as her great love has shown. But whoever has been forgiven little loves little."*

Then, He told the woman her sins were forgiven and that she could go in peace (Luke 7:48-50, NIV).

Needless to say, this astounded the other guest and made them even more captivated with Jesus.

The Pharisees were small –minded, judgmental people. They did things for show and only looked at what could be seen on the outside. To them, I'm sure it was downright blasphemous that someone would claim to be the Messiah and associate with some of the people Jesus did. Who knows what they thought was taking place when Jesus got together with some of the people He was trying to encourage, inspire, heal, redeem and give hope.

All though He knew the Pharisees thought of Him as *"a glutton, a drunkard and a friend of tax collectors and sinners"* (Luke 7:34), Jesus didn't let that stop Him from seeking out those who needed Him the most. He didn't turn anyone away *then* and He still doesn't turn anyone away *today*!

In no means can I convey in one chapter, with mere words the bold, brave, righteous, Divine and determined spirit of Jesus…the Rebel.

All I can do is offer these small examples to show you: Here is someone who did everything *perfect*. He stood up for the truth, wasn't afraid to speak His mind, loved God and only wanted to help people by sharing His message.

Yet, the "religious" people of His time still found fault with Him. They talked about where He came from, the company He kept and even the Holy work He was doing. They were obsessed with trying to discredit Jesus. So much so, they continued to watch Him, talk about Him, plot against Him, and eventually had Him arrested and crucified.

However, even their last-ditch, desperate attempt to silence Him didn't work. Jesus is alive and well! Two thousand years after He walked the Earth, His voice is still being heard!

I wanted to write this chapter to help you understand that no matter how good your intentions are, how pure your heart is or how close to God you are…there will always be people who do the same thing to you. There will always be someone who has their opinion on what you *should* do, what you *shouldn't* do, how you *should* do it or *who* you should be doing it with.

However, I want to encourage each and every one of you to find the little bit of "Jesus…the Rebel" that lives in you. Continue to move forward and represent Him in the way that's right for *you*.

Know in your heart that He understands you, loves you and will have your back every step of the way. Don't be afraid to shake things up, ruffle some feathers and do your best to make Him proud. I know I certainly will!

CHAPTER 17

INVITE GOD TO THE PARTY!

*"So whether you eat or drink or whatever you do, do it all for the glory of God", (*1 Corinthians 10:31, NIV*).*

I want to start this chapter by thanking you for taking this journey of spiritual growth with me. Looking back on these chapters and the lessons contained in them, I can remember exactly where I was in my life when God was teaching me each one. I'm grateful for the opportunity to be able to share them with you. I can guarantee that everything you've read in this book will help you in some way in your quest to grow closer to God. It certainly has made a big difference in my life!

We've talked about a lot of things, like learning to accept God's love and approval and how to become comfortable letting Him into our lives. We've discovered new and unconventional ways to do so and how a positive attitude will help us communicate with Him.

We've gone deeper and exposed the devil and his lies, his plan to attack our mind and the many tactics he uses against us. We've discussed the arsenal of spiritual weapons we have to beat him and the power and authority we have been given to put them to use. We've even talked about how fighting back and daring to believe in the power of God will help us overcome F.E.A.R and learn to enjoy our lives more.

Now, I want to encourage you to take what you've read, find what works for you and share those things with others.

Each one of us is able to make an impact in his or her own way. God made each of us with different talents, abilities, voices and opinions. Don't be afraid to let Him use those things to reach other people!

I know bringing up God and spirituality with others can be a slippery slope. It can either go really right …or really wrong. But, don't worry…I would never leave you hanging!

In this chapter, "Invite God to the Party!" I'll give you some tips on how to share what you've learned with others, start conversations and make being a believer look as cool as it really is! I'll also let you in on one very important key that has helped me in doing so. And, I'll show you how to do this without coming off as an overbearing "religious" person or sending people running for the hills in the process!

Honestly, many Christians don't make having God in your life seem like much fun. Hopefully, this chapter will help you step out and find new and exciting ways to show people otherwise. Once you do, you never know who you'll be able to help!

The first thing I want to encourage you to do when reaching out to others…is to be yourself. Psalm 139:14(NIV), assures us that we are *"fearfully and wonderfully made"* and that all of God's works are wonderful.

Don't let anyone make you feel like you can't be yourself or that you have to fit into some mold of what people think a "Christian" should be.

We just saw how Jesus didn't fit any of the religious leader's expectations for the Messiah. Yet, He was the real deal!

The world doesn't need any more "cookie –cutter" Christians. We already have enough of those. God made you to be exactly who you are and that's more than enough for Him to work with.

Isaiah 64:8 (NIV) encourages us to be ourselves by saying, *"Yet you, LORD, are our Father. We are the clay, you are the potter; we are all the work of your hand."*

Take a minute and really think about that scripture. Imagine God taking the time to specifically create each one of us like a potter creates on his wheel. That alone should make you excited and eager to be yourself!

Jeremiah 1:5 (NLT) explains, *"I knew you before I formed you in your mother's womb. Before you were born I set you apart and appointed you as my prophet to the nations."*

All you have to do is look around to see the results of God's creativity. We are all different colors, heights, sizes and shapes. We all have different abilities, personalities, talents and strengths. You have to be confidant in who God made *you* to be! After all, He can't use any of your unique qualities if you're trying to be like someone else.

1 Corinthians 12:4-6 (NLT) tells us, *"There are different kinds of spiritual gifts, but the same Spirit is the source of them all. There are different kinds of service, but we serve the same Lord. There are different kinds of working, but in all of them and in everyone it is the same God at work."*

You may look different, talk different, dress different or even worship in a different way, but that doesn't mean you're wrong. What's different and unique about you just may be what God uses to help draw someone else in!

For example, some of you may be familiar with Jan Crouch. Her and her husband, Paul Crouch, founded TBN…the Trinity Broadcasting Network in 1973. I have to admit; I wasn't that familiar with her sermons. However, I was familiar with one very unique thing about Jan…her huge pink hair!

She always wore her hair as big as she could get it and it was always some shade of cotton –candy pink.

I can recall many times surfing through the channels and having no choice but to stop and listen to this colorful lady on TV preaching about God. She always had a fire in her heart and a mountain of pink hair on top of her head.

With a style like hers, Jan was probably never afraid to be herself. She probably always stood out and was different. But, God was able to use what was different about her to draw people in. As a matter of fact, He inspired Jan and Paul to create a whole network where people could be drawn in by her uniqueness!

Can you imagine how many people Jan Crouch probably helped lead to the Lord just by them stopping and listening because of her hairstyle alone? That may not have happened if she was trying to be anyone other than herself.

God can take that one thing about us that stands *out* and use it to help others stand *up*. That's just what He did with Jan.

Even though both Jan and Paul have passed away, their legacy continues to live on. Their television network, TBN continues to be one of the most watched faith networks for millions of Christians around the world. Even though they are gone, their influence is still helping lead people to God every day. See, you never know what type of impact you could have by just being yourself!

Many people think Christians are all the same. They think we all dress alike, talk alike, act alike and are missing any real personality except for worshiping or judgment. It's time for us to show them different!

So, I encourage you to find out what's different and unique about you and let God use it. Are you comical, smart, passionate, loud, artistic or talkative? Are you a "people" person, a good listener, a writer, have a cool style, a great singing voice or some other unique quality?

Whatever it is, I guarantee there will be someone who is drawn to it and you'll have the opportunity to give God the glory!

Once we understand that it's okay to be ourselves, the next step in reaching out to others with our faith…is learning to keep it real.

The world is a difficult place to live today. It's very tense and getting harder for people to maintain peace, motivation, positivity and faith. People need to see Christians they can relate to.

They need to know that the same strength, grace, favor and hope we've been given to make it through life is available to them as well. They need to know that the same forgiveness, mercy and unconditional love that covers us protects them too.

However, there are some Christians who don't convey that message very well. Some Christians try to hide their flaws behind a perfect image and act like they never need any of those things.

Acting like we're perfect, never mess up, don't struggle, fall short or sin is unrealistic. Who can relate to someone like that?

It makes us look like hypocrites (just like the Pharisees). It does nothing to draw others in, encourage them, give them hope or make them want to know more about what we believe in. In fact, it does the complete opposite!

To any Christian who feels they have to put up a perfect front, please understand this; you are only chasing people away! People are tired of phoniness and are searching for something *real*. Even kids are growing up quicker, smarter and more intuitive than ever before. They can spot something fake a mile away.

These type of Christians, (who I call "perfect- praisers") need to realize that they may be able to fool some *people* and may even be able to fool *themselves*, but there's someone they will *never* be able to fool… and that's God, He created us and knows everything about us. That includes the good, the bad and everything in –between!

Hebrews 4:13(NLT), reminds us, *"Nothing in all creation is hidden from God. Everything is naked and exposed before his eyes, and he is the one to whom we are accountable."*

In Jeremiah 23:24 (NASB), the Lord asks, *"Can a man hide himself in hiding places so I do not see him?" declares the Lord. 'Do I not fill the heavens and the earth?' declares the Lord."*

And, Psalms 139:1-6(GNT) reads, *"Lord, you have examined me and you know me. You know everything I do; from far away you understand all my thoughts. You see me, whether I am working or resting; you know all my actions. Even before I speak, you already know what I will say. You are all around me on every side: you protect me with your power. Your knowledge of me is too deep; it is beyond my understanding."*

Once we understand that we can never fool God and that He is not impressed by perfect behavior… we can relax. We can take the pressure off ourselves and others as well.

If God *Himself* sees our worst behavior, forgives us and still loves us unconditionally, why should anyone, especially Christians, feel the need to try and fool others? Aren't we supposed to be testaments to God's love, grace, favor, mercy and forgiveness?

Keeping it real helps us be relatable and authentic. That's what people are looking for!

No matter if they're attending a church service full of thousands or reading an inspirational quote on their Facebook page, people want to know who they're listening to is *real*.

There are very few things in life that are perfect and we shouldn't feel like we have to be one of them. More importantly, we shouldn't make other people feel like they have to be either!

The next thing I want to encourage you to do when reaching out to others with your faith is to let them see you actually *enjoying* your relationship with God. I mean, enjoying The Lord's presence is one of the best things about having Him in our life, right?

Yet, somewhere along the line, I think many Christians have forgotten that aspect of the relationship. Some even look at their relationship with the Lord as a burden. They begin to think of spending time with God as an obligation rather than a privilege. That probably explains why some of them are so miserable!

How can we encourage others to want to take part in what we believe in …if they don't see us enjoying it ourselves?

Spending time with the Lord should be fun. I know many people don't think those two things go hand in hand, but they do! However, how *much* they do…depends on you.

I think people forget that Jesus was cool. They let His enormous and awesome purpose overshadow that aspect of Him.

He was a social person. He enjoyed having dinner at people's homes. He enjoyed good food, wine and company. He enjoyed get-togethers, traveling and meeting all different types of people. He hung out with an interesting group of disciples who, despite their many hang-ups, were good people as well. He liked to have fun and laugh.

He was the perfect mix of social and spiritual. People *wanted* to be around Him!

Hebrews 13:8(NIV) tells us, *"Jesus Christ is the same yesterday and today and forever."* So, none of that has changed. However, too many people don't get to experience the fun side of the Lord because they won't take him out of the "Sunday morning box" they keep Him in. The scripture tells us Jesus is:

- *"A friend that will stick closer than a brother"* (Proverbs 18:24), yet many people push Him away until it's time for church.
- *"He is our advocate in all situations"* (1 John 2:1), yet some only think of Him when they're in trouble.
- *"He is a provider"* (Philippians 4:19), yet some only think of the material things He can offer.

We have to stop doing that. We need to start thinking of our relationship with the Lord just like that of a best friend. They know everything about us. They know our likes, dislikes, insecurities, secrets, strengths, weaknesses, goals and dreams. They know all the good things about us, all the bad things about us, all the mistakes we've made and we never have to worry about their opinion of us changing because of any of it.

We look forward to hanging out with them, laughing, having a good time and can completely relax around them. That relationship is easy because they "get" us. Well, I can tell you this …no one will ever "get" you more than God!

So, make an effort to include Him in the fun areas of your life. Loosen up and learn to "Invite God to the Party!" He likes to have fun too!

Do what it says to do in Ecclesiastes 9:7(NLT), *"So go ahead. Eat your food with joy, and drink your wine with a happy heart, for God approves of this!"*

Ecclesiastes 8:15(NLT) also reads, *"So I recommend having fun, because there is nothing better for people in this world than to eat, drink, and enjoy life. That way they will experience some happiness along with all the hard work God gives them under the sun."*

The more people see us enjoying our relationship with the Lord, the more eager they'll be to find out how to have that same type of relationship for themselves! It doesn't make them feel looked down upon or judged when you reach out to them .It helps them see that you can have God in your life, still have fun, laugh, be yourself and enjoy the things He put here for us to enjoy!

There is one more tip I want to share with you when reaching out to others. This one is crucial in order for *any* of this to work. It could mean the difference between drawing others in or sending them running in the opposite direction.

When you decide to make God a part of your life, it's really easy to get overwhelmed. The experience is so awesome that you want to dive in and give it your all.

However, I bet we all know someone who has made God a part of his or her life… and then completely went off the deep end. They go around scrutinizing what everyone else does, they can't open their mouth without a scripture flying out, they have a laundry list of things they can no longer do and they pretty much make everyone around them miserable.

We've all seen movies where the Christian is portrayed as the "religious nut", the "Jesus freak" or some other type of Bible –toting weirdo.

Well, how do we make God a part of our life, represent our faith and reach out to others without coming off as that type of person?

The answer is simple…balance.

I can't tell you how important balance is to representing God the right way.

Proverbs 11:1 tells us, *"A false balance is an abomination to the LORD, but a just weight is his delight."* In order to be taken seriously, we can't lean too far in any direction.

Ecclesiastes 7:18(NIV) speaks on that by saying, *"It is good to grasp the one and not let go of the other. Whoever fears God will avoid all extremes."*

You don't want to be seen as someone who *only* goes to church, who can *only* talk about the Bible, who *only* tells people what they're doing wrong.

It's important that people see Christians as well-balanced individuals with lives, interest, hobbies, personalities and other things going on.

Ecclesiastes 7:16(NASB) warns us, *"Do not be excessively righteous and do not be overly wise. Why should you ruin yourself?"*

An unbalanced Christian can do a world of damage to the Kingdom of God. Oftentimes, they're so overbearing that their attempts to show others how awesome it is to have God in your life completely backfire.

I remember one time in particular where I saw this happen and was faced with a decision to make.

One day, I was at work and one of my close friends, Corey, was sitting at his desk behind me. Corey is a cool guy, and we've been friends for many years. At this point we were just getting to know each other. We would go to lunch together, talk about movies, music, girls and would hang out at each other's apartment playing video games.

Corey is the type of person who likes to question *everything*. He loves to debate things and has to know the who, what, when, where, how and why behind any subject. It's just one of the things that makes him who he is. I've learned that about him and I sort of get a kick out of it.

This particular day, Corey was sitting beside a girl who worked with us named Robin. Robin was nice, friendly and a little bit older than us. They were talking and the topic of religion came up. I wasn't really listening, but this caught my attention. I knew Robin was a Christian, like myself and I knew Corey had his doubts and questions about the subject. I thought to myself, *"Well…this should be interesting."*

So, I listened as I continued to work. Almost immediately, they started disagreeing. Robin would bring up reasons why everyone should believe in God, and Corey would come up with something to dispute it. Robin would talk about the Bible and Corey would question it. Corey would demand proof that God existed and Robin would hit him over the head with scripture after scripture. This went on for a while.

Then, Corey asked her, "Am I supposed to believe that there is somebody sitting up in the sky watching all of us, controlling everything we do?"

Well, this caused Robin to go into Super -Christian mode. She went off on him so hard that I thought she was going to catch the Holy Ghost, start speaking in tongues and roll around on the floor! Finally, Corey just threw his hands up in frustration and said, "Just forget it…I don't even believe in God!"

Now, keep in mind I was hanging out with this guy and we were becoming good friends. I knew he had some speculation and questions about spirituality, but I didn't think it went *that* deep.

I knew that he was a good guy and it was just part of his personality to question everything. However, he said this so adamantly, that my first thought was, *"What…you don't believe in God? Well, I can't be your friend anymore."*

Immediately, God spoke to me and said, *"Yes, you can. You may be the only balanced version of Me he ever sees. To stop being his friend because of what he said would only push him further away."*

I was glad to hear that because I don't befriend just anyone and I knew Corey was a good person. Plus, I enjoyed hanging out with him.

I'm not sure how the conversation went after that. It was at a standstill so I tuned it out. All I knew was the way Robin was going about it wasn't going to be winning any souls that day.

Afterward, I continued my friendship with Corey as usual. For weeks, I didn't mention that I had heard the conversation he had with Robin. One night we were hanging out and I decided to bring it up.

I never kept my spirituality a secret and Corey knew that I believed in God.

However, when I told him what I heard him say, he immediately got a funny look on his face and said, "Man… it's not that I *don't* believe in God, but every time I have a different opinion, question something or look at things a different way, most Christians start throwing the Bible at me. It's like they're trying to force me to believe. It's not that I have anything against believing in God but what I don't like is the way some Christians act when they are trying to get you to believe. It makes me not want any part of it."

All I could think was, *"Okay, now I get it."* Here was a good friend of mine, who I thought was closed off to having God in his life, but was actually turned off because of how some Christians were acting.

It was in his nature to question everything. However, if all someone did when he had questions was throw a bunch of scriptures at him and act "holier than thou" when he had his own ideas…of course he was going to run in the opposite direction.

RIGHTEOUSNESS, THE REMIX- TURN UP THE VOLUME ON GOD!

Corey needed to see someone living it, not just talking about it. He had to see how believing in God was practical in everyday life. He had to be shown the meanings behind the scriptures ...not just hit over the head with them.

Then, I understood how important it was that I remained his friend. I realized how important it was for him to see a Christian who wasn't trying to beat him over the head with their beliefs every chance they got.

This took place years ago. I remained friends with Corey and am still good friends with him today.

He's always seen me doing everything we're talking about in this chapter. I've always been myself, kept it real, enjoyed my relationship with God and made it a part of my life in a balanced way. I hope by doing so, he has seen a more fun, cool and accepting side of God that he can relate to.

That was just *one* instance but this sort of thing happens all the time. I've come across many people who say they don't feel comfortable opening up, asking questions about God, going to church or pursuing their own spirituality because of the way some Christians act.

I've heard people say they're afraid of being judged or looked down upon.

That incident was a great learning experience for me. It taught me to be mindful in my approach. There's nothing wrong with being passionate about your beliefs. There's nothing wrong with being on fire for the Lord and expressing that to others. However, every job doesn't require a bulldozer!

Seeing how Robin handled that situation with Corey was like watching someone use a sledgehammer to swat a fly. It was just too much.

Ecclesiastes 3:1-8(NIV) tells us, *"There is a time for everything, and a season for every activity under the heavens: a time to be born and a time to die, a time to plant and a time to uproot, a time to kill and a time to heal, a time to tear down and a time to build, a time to weep and a time to laugh, a time to mourn and a time to dance, a time to scatter stones and a time to gather them, a time to embrace and a time to refrain from embracing, a time to search and a time to give up, a time to keep and a time to throw away, a time to tear and a time to mend, a time to be silent and a time to speak, a time to love and a time to hate, a time for war and a time for peace."*

So yes, there are times when we absolutely have to stand up for our beliefs, be unyielding and not back down. However, there are also times when we have to meet others where they are with a little more understanding, acceptance and patience.

Finding the right balance is important when reaching out to people. It could mean the difference between someone deciding to believe or breaking their neck to get away from you!

That's part of the reason I wanted to write this book. I wanted to show those who are hesitant to let God into their life that there's more than one type of believer.

I mean, look at me, I haven't stepped foot in a church since I was a teenager. Yet, I was able to get alone with God and make Him a big enough part of my life where He was able to show me all the things you read in this book.

I wanted to show other Christians just because someone doesn't choose to build their relationship with God in church doesn't mean they're any less spiritual, wise or less connected to Him than anyone else.

As long as you accept Jesus into your life, know that He died for your sins and accept His sacrifice…the rest is up to you and Him. There's no blueprint for how that relationship should play out.

That's the exciting part! We are all connected to God in our own unique way. So, go ahead, dive right in and develop that relationship.

Use what you've learned in this book to build your spirituality if you're just starting out or to strengthen it if you're already on your path. Use what you've read in this chapter to encourage others to do the same.

Turn up the Volume on God and see what He has to say. You may just be surprised. I know I was!

ABOUT THE AUTHOR

O. Redd is one-third of the Virginia based rap group, Young, Fly & Dangerous. They specialize in party music and have been nominated for numerous awards and recognized for their high energy stage performances. He has been writing music, performing and pursuing his passion since his teens. Recently, he decided to expand his writing ability to include the publication of his first book, Turn Up the Volume on God, in order to share the faith he has developed along the way. Redd is also an aspiring actor and motivational speaker. For booking information, contact Oreddtheremix@gmail.com or connectwithredd.com.